Mary Baker Eddy
and Her Books

MARY BAKER EDDY
as she appeared in 1880

MARY BAKER EDDY AND HER BOOKS

WILLIAM DANA ORCUTT

THE CHRISTIAN SCIENCE PUBLISHING SOCIETY
BOSTON, MASSACHUSETTS, U. S. A.

ISBN: 0-87510-274-3
Library of Congress Catalog Card No.: 91-73361

PRINTED IN THE UNITED STATES OF AMERICA

INTRODUCTION
"Twentieth-Century Biographers Series"

In the closing years of the twentieth century, there is a growing awareness that the hundred years since 1900 will have registered a magnitude and pace of change, in every aspect of human affairs, which probably exceeds any historic precedent. In political, social and religious institutions and attitudes, in the sciences and industry, in the arts, in how we communicate with each other, humanity has traveled light years in this century.

"Earth's actors," said the Founder of Christian Science, Mary Baker Eddy, "change earth's scenes . . . ." As we look back over the landscape of this century, some towering figures emerge into view: political leaders, scientists and inventors, authors, artists and musicians, social and religious pioneers, industrialists, and many others who helped "change earth's scenes."

Typically, when someone comes along who changes human perceptions and ways of acting he or she attracts biographers. If an individual career is perceived, with growing distance, to have been especially significant in its impact on human affairs and changing ideas, the shelf of biography steadily expands; and each new published work, even though it may cover some of the ground already treated in earlier works, is expected to bring further insight into the meaning of a life, a mind, and a career.

INTRODUCTION

Even among those who are not her followers, Mary Baker Eddy is customarily regarded as a major religious figure of the twentieth century and as a notable example of the emergence of women in significant leadership roles. Her works are visible today in virtually every country of the world: in church buildings, in Christian Science Reading Rooms, in the distribution of the newspaper and religious periodicals she established and their derivative broadcast forms, in the wide circulation of her own writings and, most important, in the way hundreds of thousands of people conduct their everyday lives.

Public interest in Mrs. Eddy, and curiosity about her, are as strong today as they were in 1910, the year of her decease. And yet, compared with other major figures of the century, the shelf of biography has increased little in the intervening years. A handful of early biographies, by those who knew her or stood close to her in time, were augmented in the late 1960s by Robert Peel's monumental three-volume work. Most of those early works, in spite of their great value as part of the historical record, have lapsed from print; and in fact some firsthand reminiscences by individuals who worked directly with her have only been privately published or circulated.

As we near the close of a century which directly witnessed some of Mary Baker Eddy's major contributions, The Christian Science Publishing Society, the publishing arm of the church she established, has been asked to reexamine the church's obligations to future generations and centuries, in providing an appreciation and understanding of her remarkable career.

Mrs. Eddy wrote only briefly about herself, in a short volume titled *Retrospection and Introspection.* She discouraged personal adulation or attention, clearly hoping that people would find her character and purpose in her own writings rather than in the biographic record. Yet, she came to see the need for an accurate account of her life and gave specific if possibly reluctant acquiescence in the year 1910 to the publishing of the first of the biographies — Sybil Wilbur's *Mary Baker Eddy.*

In addition to Robert Peel's trilogy, which is still in print, a number of significant biographic resources must remain, or become, permanently and readily available to future generations. These include: firsthand recollections of early workers who served directly under her leadership, not all of which have yet been published; and the various biographies which have already won their place in the history of Christian Science and in public use.

For these reasons, the Publishing Society welcomes the opportunity of publishing, and keeping in print, a major shelf of works on Mary Baker Eddy under the general series title: "Twentieth-Century Biographers Series."

Although a consistent set of editorial standards has been applied to such elements as indexing and footnoting, where required, with regard to dates, events, and statements of fact, the original texts of the authors have been preserved intact.

INTRODUCTION

If the reader finds, through these volumes, occasional differing interpretations of events or concepts, this should serve as a strength rather than a weakness in a record which is so clearly synoptical in nature. Especially in the case of those who worked directly with Mrs. Eddy and shared many of her experiences, a special measure of respect and textual integrity is demanded. These are the workers she chose — individuals who served as her lieutenants, often for many years. To describe them as sturdy, strong-minded workers, patriarchal in their devotion and self-sacrifice, scarcely does them justice.

Mrs. Eddy's career and works have stirred humanity in the twentieth century and will continue to do so. Perhaps an appropriate introduction for this series is captured in her statement, in the Preface to *Science and Health:* "The time for thinkers has come." In that spirit, this series of biographies by many different twentieth-century writers is offered to all those who, now and in the future, want to know more about this remarkable woman, her life, and her work.

PUBLISHER'S NOTE

WHEN *Willliam Dana Orcutt delivered to The Christian Science Publishing Society the manuscript of this book, he said, with the deep reverence which has characterized all his dealings with Mary Baker Eddy and her published works, that if he had chosen a text for this new book it would have been the statement of the Discoverer and Founder of Christian Science: "The divinity of the Christ was made manifest in the humanity of Jesus" (Science and Health with Key to the Scriptures, p. 25).*

While Mr. Orcutt does not profess himself to be a follower of the great religious movement established by Mary Baker Eddy, it is not alone his profound respect for her and for the blessings which she bestowed upon humanity that commends him as the author of this book. It is also the fact that he is eminently qualified to record accurately and impartially many phases of her career and of her service to her fellow men which have not previously come to light. He has also authenticated and confirmed the magnificence and deep spirituality of the great Leader of the Christian Science denomination, and he has done this in a manner which is at once unique and inspiring.

William Dana Orcutt is known as one of the

PUBLISHER'S NOTE

world's great makers of books, as the author of many books, and as the writer of delightful essays in The Christian Science Monitor. *Of his novels, "Changing Patterns" and "The Spell" were perhaps the most widely read. His books on books are recognized as classics in their field, and include "In Quest of the Perfect Book" and "The Book in Italy." First editions of Orcutt volumes are collectors' items.*

Mr. Orcutt lived in Boston and on Cape Cod, and his was one of the famous families of old New England. Through the years he found time for travel and study in many countries. Few contemporaries equalled his world-wide acquaintance with the great men and women of arts and letters during the closing years of the 19th century and the first fifty years of the 20th century. His reminiscences of experiences with these personages were published on the editorial page of The Christian Science Monitor *and afterwards appeared in book form under the title "Celebrities Off Parade."*

CONTENTS

Foreword

Foreword

WITH the exception of the Holy Bible, the Christian Science textbook, "Science and Health with Key to the Scriptures" by Mary Baker Eddy, holds every printing and publishing record. Written by an unknown author, privately printed in 1875 without benefit of publishers' promotion or even booksellers' interest, this volume has gone through hundreds of editions, comprising several million copies, bought by individuals all over the world. The word "bought" is used advisedly, for Science and Health has always been and is today bought rather than sold. Practically, Science and Health is still privately published, the business details being handled by a Publishers' Agent, acting for the Trustees under the Will of Mary Baker Eddy, and then sold and distributed through more than three thousand Christian Science Reading Rooms located throughout the world.

Another record is the fact that, with the exception of the first two editions, which were liabilities rather than assets to the author because of incompetent manufacture, the printing of the various editions from 1881 down to the present time has been in the hands of but two printers, with both of whom Mrs. Eddy established and maintained a degree of friendship which

[3]

could not fail to affect the harmony and the consistency which characterized the editions during that period. John Wilson was Mrs. Eddy's manufacturer from 1881 to 1897, when he retired from the University Press at Cambridge, Massachusetts, and, as his understudy and successor as head of that famous institution, I happily inherited this responsibility in 1897, and continued the service throughout Mrs. Eddy's lifetime, and down to the present moment. And, to establish a final and most impressive record, I know of no instance during this long business association of nearly seventy years, of any business misunderstanding.

I first met Mrs. Eddy at her home, Pleasant View, Concord, New Hampshire, in the summer of 1892, when I served as Mr. Wilson's representative and messenger in connection with the edition of Science and Health running through the Press at that time; my last personal conference with her was in April, 1910, when she called me to her Chestnut Hill home in a suburb of Boston to consult with her concerning the proposed manufacture of her Poems. During those years I had a wonderful opportunity to see, firsthand, her consummate ability to assume and carry through the countless business details without permitting them to divert her from her concentration upon the unfolding of her message. The responsibility of the publishing and distribution of the first forty-eight editions fell entirely on her except insofar as John Wilson and the

University Press assisted her, beyond the relations nor-
mally existing between printer and author. I was personally a participant from this point on. I saw the
efforts Mrs. Eddy made to gain relief from business
details by the appointment of her first publisher, William
G. Nixon, and became aware of how completely he
failed her. I was thrown closely with her second publisher, Dr. E. J. Foster-Eddy, and was called upon to
correct omissions and commissions resulting from his
indifference and inefficiency. All this made my visits
to Pleasant View more frequent, and even then, as a
young man unacquainted with the countless other disturbing influences beyond those which aroused indignation at the University Press, I marveled at the
calmness and serenity with which Mrs. Eddy met
every problem it was my duty to report to her; the
directness with which she settled every question, and
her ever-present consideration for others. She had no
words of censure for anyone. Her regret was that
Mr. Wilson had been put to extra trouble, and she was
grateful for his wholehearted co-operation. From all
these diverting disturbances, she was able to turn back
to her spiritual tasks without the slightest outward sign
of interruption. It was an amazing exhibition of inward
control that the practical demands could be so completely disassociated from her definite mission without
impairing either one.

A study of the obstacles placed in the way of the

author by disloyal friends, jealous associates, and a hos-
tile, prejudiced public, much of which I had ample
opportunity to witness personally, could not fail to
convince the most violent skeptic that the book Science
and Health was bound to be issued, and that the message
the author was undertaking to convey to the world
was not to be and could not be suppressed.

In this narrative I have tried to show Mrs. Eddy as
she remains in my mind after all this period. During
the eighteen years my business duties brought me in
contact with her I did not fully realize how deeply her
generous interest and wise counsels were affecting my
professional career; looking back, I may say that except
for this interest I should never have remained in the
profession of making or designing books. She impressed
on me the real dignity that belongs to the printer, if
he himself recognizes it. This volume may be taken,
then, as a slight token of acknowledgment and gratitude.

In recording actual conversations, I have not hesitated to use direct quotations. After so many years I
could make no claim to *verbatim* accuracy, but I can
state definitely that I believe the words I have employed
correctly convey the meaning Mrs. Eddy intended to
express. Anyone who ever talked with her will bear
me out in saying that it was easier to remember what
she said than to forget it. Mrs. Eddy wasted few words
in general conversation. When she spoke, it was to
express a well-conceived and well-constructed idea;

when she listened, it was usually to receive the reaction
to a thought she had already advanced. Her features
were unusually expressive, changing constantly with
the change in subject, and I am impressed by the fact
that as I record a conversation with her I seem to
associate with it the various phases that were reflected
in her face.

Someone once said, "Heaven on earth is the re-
enactment of our fondest memories." I have been
reminded of this as I have written the pages of this
book.

W. D. O.

PART I

Mrs. Eddy and John Wilson

1881 - 1897

Mrs. Eddy and John Wilson
1881 - 1897

I HEARD John Wilson repeat so many times the story of his earliest business association with Mary Baker Eddy that I feel almost as if I had been present personally. It was on an afternoon in January, 1881, when this slight, unassuming woman presented herself at the door of the counting room of the University Press in Cambridge, Massachusetts, and asked to see Mr. Wilson. I say "counting room," as it was never called "office" in those days, being as English in layout as if located in old London itself. As Mrs. Eddy entered she would have found the clerks and the bookkeepers sitting on high stools, wearing skullcaps and long, black, alpaca coats. Mr. Wilson would have been sitting at a table, on which he wrote all business letters by hand.

Mr. Wilson at that time was included with Theodore L. DeVinne and Henry O. Houghton as one of the three outstanding book manufacturers in America. His father was the original John Wilson in the firm of John Wilson and Son, and the present John was the original son. Born in Manchester, England, of an English mother and a Scottish father, this John had come to

America with his parents as a youth, had served his apprenticeship under his father in Boston; and, after the elder Wilson's passing, had acquired the plant of the University Press in Cambridge from the one-time owners, Welch, Bigelow & Company.

Here the present John produced books of a quality that added luster to the already established reputation of the old University Press, the lineal descendant of the Stephen Daye Press, the first printing establishment set up in British North America. Here in 1640, the Bay Psalm Book had been printed, and in 1663 the Eliot Indian Bible; here in more modern days had been manufactured the epoch-making volumes of Oliver Wendell Holmes, Jared Sparks, William Hickling Prescott, John Gorham Palfrey, Josiah Quincy, Edward Everett, Richard Henry Dana, Henry Wadsworth Longfellow, Nathaniel Hawthorne, John Greenleaf Whittier, Ralph Waldo Emerson, Benjamin H. Tichnor, and James Russell Lowell. Little did John Wilson realize, that January afternoon, that the modest but confident little woman sitting at his desk was about to hand him the manuscript of a future classic which, in popularity, sales, and influence upon the world, would outrival the writings of any of the famous authors who had preceded her!

John Wilson, the father, started his career as a printer at Kilmarnock in Scotland. An intimate friend of the poet Robert Burns, in 1786 he issued the first edition of Burns' poems. He was a deeply religious man, but of exactly what sect I have never been able to determine, in spite of perusing over a thousand hand-written pages of an unpublished theological volume he wrote on Angelology, which at one time fell into my hands. John Wilson, the son, called his father, in the Scottish accent he never wholly lost, "an advanced Unitarian, but regardless of sect, a verra Godly man," and throughout his life sought to live up to the precepts he inherited. I mention this as it is undoubtedly one reason why Mrs. Eddy so promptly excited his interest and secured his co-operation.

Although strangers, this was not the first time Mr. Wilson and Mrs. Eddy had met. Three years earlier, when she was frustrated in her efforts to put the second [Ark] edition of Science and Health through the press, her husband, Asa G. Eddy, had called Mr. Wilson in for advice in the dilemma. Mr. Wilson responded by going over with her the confused mass of proof, on which Mrs. Eddy had struggled to correct the countless errors occasioned by the carelessness of the printer, and showed her how about 170 pages could be salvaged. This, while not repairing the damage done by the poor workmanship, at least provided the author with the slight little Volume II which served to bridge the gap until the third edition could be manufactured. Mr. Wilson had long since forgotten this friendly act, but

Mrs. Eddy never forgot a kindness. She made up her mind at that time that when the third edition was ready for the press, John Wilson should be the printer.

In April, 1880, there was correspondence between Mr. Eddy and John Wilson concerning the third edition. Evidently the specifications were not made quite clear, so Mr. Wilson wrote Mr. Eddy on April 3:

Before giving you an estimate we should like to know exactly what is required. How many *new* pages are to be set up; how many pages are already set up and stereotyped; what quality of paper do you wish, — paper having advanced in price.

Science and Health makes now we think, some 130 pages. If so, your intention is, if we understand your note, to add some 270 pages to this book.

When you let us know, we shall be most happy to give you (our) figures. We should require one-half of the amount before commencing the work.

Nothing came of this correspondence, undoubtedly because Mrs. Eddy was unable to advance one half the cost of the proposed new edition. At all events, she evidently decided to present the case in person, and this explained her presence at the University Press that January afternoon in 1881. She recalled herself to Mr. Wilson, and he responded sympathetically as she related her experience. The earlier meeting had been to him the story of an authoress in distress; the present problem became a responsibility to restore her faith in printers.

Mrs. Eddy herself was a far more effective advocate for printing the new edition of her book than her husband could possibly have been. Mr. Wilson was a very impressionable man, and what Mrs. Eddy had to tell him of her experiences with printers, and what he had personally seen three years before, would be a far more determining reason for giving her credit than any argument Mr. Eddy might have advanced. At their earlier meeting, Mr. Wilson heard the story only of the second edition — at this time she explained in detail all that had happened.

Even during a conference that extended throughout that afternoon in January, 1881, Mrs. Eddy could not have begun to tell Mr. Wilson the whole story of the unhappy incidents associated with the first two editions as we know them today from the biographers' revelations. Mrs. Eddy had brought with her the first and second editions of Science and Health as exhibits. In the earliest printing there were literally hundreds of typographical mistakes, which distorted and confused the meaning. This would have been bad enough in any volume, but in a book of the nature of Science and Health such inaccuracies absolutely affected its usefulness.

Except for the careless proofreading, the first two editions were well enough made to pass muster among the volumes turned out by printers of that period, during which printing was carried on as a trade rather than as an art. W. F. Brown & Company, of Boston, who

made the first edition, were job rather than book printers, and the ornamental type used in display was of
course entirely out of keeping with the subject matter,
being better suited for use in circulars, flyers, and
broadsides which these printers were accustomed to
print. Mrs. Eddy had begun the actual writing of
Science and Health in February, 1872, and the manuscript of all but one chapter went to the printers in
September, 1874. The manufacture required over a
year, owing to the fact that the work on the book
came to a stop whenever the author's advance pay-
ments became exhausted. When finally issued in 1875
(456 pages), the type was not too worn, the presswork
was not too uneven, the binding was not too bad; it
was simply a commonplace, undistinguished example
of its time. But the proofreading was simply atrocious!

And there was more to it than the typographical
errors, bad as they were. From the very beginning of
her writing Mrs. Eddy made such use of words as to
give them a special meaning. This was carried out
consistently and effectively by the author, but the
printer officiously took it upon himself to "correct"
many such instances. When Mrs. Eddy discovered
this unwarranted liberty taken with her original copy,
she laboriously undertook to make the changes in the
plates themselves to save the expense of new plates.
"I have now the part of proofreader to take," she records
in a letter, "or my book will be spoiled. . . . I now

have to count the letters of every word I take out or insert when I make corrections."

The second edition Mr. Wilson had already seen. Its printers, Rand, Avery & Company, in Boston, were also far more experienced in job work than in printing books. Considered as an example of the bookmaking of the 1870's, it was not far enough below standard to excite comment, but again, and inexcusably, the proofreading was wretched.

Nothing aroused John Wilson's indignation so quickly as poor proofreading. He regarded a book as the vehicle of a message, and to have the delivery of that message frustrated by the inaccuracy of the vehicle was something he could not tolerate. I well remember, when I assumed my position as proofreader at the University Press in the summer of 1890, being greeted by a sign hanging over my desk, which read, "Eternal vigilance is the price of good proofreading." Mr. Wilson became more and more interested as Mrs. Eddy unfolded her story. The six years which had elapsed between the first edition of her work and the moment of her visit, she explained, which should have been wholly devoted to the continuing study and interpretation of the message God had given her to deliver to the world, had been slowed down by the enforced correction of her printed text. She had now completed this work, adding much new material, and it was her fervent hope that this, the third edition, might be

properly manufactured, as she knew it would be if
Mr. Wilson would accept the order.

Mr. Wilson at this point of the story always emphasized the amazing courage of this woman in meeting
the difficulties which had beset her on all sides. Not
only must she demonstrate the underlying truth of her
philosophy against almost universal opposition, but she
must translate that philosophy into words so clear and
unmistakable that its teachings could be made effective
by others beyond her personal effort. A textbook was
absolutely indispensable, and that textbook must express
with fidelity the message the author was attempting to
convey. I doubt if John Wilson absorbed many of
Mrs. Eddy's religious doctrines during that early conference, although he later became distinctly interested
in Christian Science, but during that long afternoon
he did receive an indelible impression of a great spirit,
and a faith in Mrs. Eddy's unwavering devotion to her
destiny that always characterized their long friendship.
He used to say, "Mrs. Eddy somehow makes everyone
she meets eager to co-operate."

Then, at last, they arrived at the crucial point. It
was necessary, Mrs. Eddy told him, for her to explain
to him the financial plight in which she found herself,
which was worse, even, than when her husband wrote.
As stated in Mr. Eddy's letter, she had expected to use
in the third edition 130 pages taken from the 167 pages
of the Ark edition, and to supply about 270 pages of

new copy. Now it would be necessary to incur the expense of resetting and making new plates of this reprinted matter, as the printers, without her consent, had destroyed all the plates immediately after printing the second edition. Mrs. Eddy admitted frankly that while she could pay perhaps a few hundred dollars on account, she could not possibly advance half the cost as Mr. Wilson had insisted in his letter to her husband. Her only income came from her teaching and from the tenants to whom she rented a part of her house at 8 Broad Street, in Lynn, Massachusetts. If this third edition were produced as she believed Mr. Wilson would produce it, she was confident that she could sell enough copies to meet the cost, but she could not pay in full on delivery.

Mr. Wilson never explained, even to himself, his reaction to Mrs. Eddy's appeal. From a business standpoint there was every reason to decline the whole proposition. "Yet," he would say, after frankly admitting the situation, "there wasn't a moment's hesitation in my acceptance of that order. I *knew* that the bill would be paid, and I found myself actually eager to undertake the manufacture."

He inquired when the manuscript would be ready. Mrs. Eddy reached into her handbag and produced it, completely finished, ready for the printer.

"You brought this on the chance of my accepting it?" John Wilson asked, surprised.

Mrs. Eddy smiled. "No," she replied, "not on a chance. I never doubted."

Thus in the old record book of the University Press, in which Mr. Wilson entered the orders as they were received from 1864 until he entrusted the records to me in 1892, is the entry:

𝕺𝖗𝖉𝖊𝖗𝖘 𝕽𝖊𝖈𝖊𝖎𝖛𝖊𝖉 𝖋𝖔𝖗 𝕻𝖗𝖎𝖓𝖙𝖎𝖓𝖌.

1881

DATE.

Jan. 31   X Science & Health

Mrs. Mary Baker Glover Eddy

8, Broad St

Lynn, Mass.

The new edition passed duly through the various departments of the University Press, which were modernized up to the moment — yet today they would seem ridiculously archaic. Suppose we follow the manuscript into the composition department. I like to call it Type Town, because the room was laid out like a town, with its Main Street and its side streets, running east and west, the demarcations being made with type cases on frames. It was all hand-composition in those days — linotypes or monotypes were still to come. Down Main Street were set up the correction stones, and then, in each side street or alley, were located four to eight hand-compositors, sitting back to back on stools.

Each alley was presided over by an experienced typesetter. He was the one who received from the foreman the copy that was to be set, distributed the copy, collected the proofs, and turned them over to the proofreading department. The foreman was king of his domain. No one, even in the counting room, undertook to give him orders. The compositors were girls or women, and sometimes boys. They made from $8.00 to $12.00 a week, and the man in charge of the alley made $16.00 a week, with about $4.00 extra in "fat" from his rake-off on the work that was done by the compositors in his alley. The foreman received about $25.00 a week.

There was one quality existing then which is not frequently found today — a great pride in workmanship. I remember, when one of my oldest typographers passed away, I went to the funeral services, and afterward returned home with his widow. On a table in the living room was a copy of Wentworth's Geometry — just an ordinary schoolbook. The widow picked it up and said with great pride in her voice, "Jim set every page of this book with his own hands." It was a family heirloom.

Then the galley went to the proofreading department. Proofreaders were highly educated, and far more than mere proofreaders in those days. They were editors. It was their function to discover errors inadvertently made by the authors as well as typographical mistakes, and to be ready to consult with the authors on any point that might arise. Authors would go directly up the winding stairs to the proofreading department, and spend an hour or two discussing some literary point in their manuscript, asking and receiving advice from the proofreader. In my day I remember James Russell Lowell, Edward Everett Hale, and William Dean Howells among those who availed themselves of this privilege. This was how Mrs. Eddy came to know the Rev. James Henry Wiggin, who was to assist her in the revision of later editions. After the last correction was made from the proof, the type pages were sent to the foundry for casting into stereotype or electrotype plates.

On the other side of the University Press building was the cylinder pressroom. The cylinder press was a French invention. In 1875, Mr. Welch, of Welch, Bigelow & Company, John Wilson's predecessors, brought back with him from France the first machine of this type to come into America. By 1890, the time I first remember, there had been a general acceptance of the cylinder press, but the first cylinder pressroom in America had been installed at the University Press.

It was on one of these machines that the third edition of Science and Health was printed. As the University Press had no bindery of its own, this portion of the manufacture was performed by O. J. Rand & Company on Milk Street, Boston. The Rand concern was later acquired by Mr. Wilson's sister-in-law and nephews, and, operating under the name of N. Wilson & Company, bound successive editions of Mrs. Eddy's books.

All this was eleven years before I became a part of the University Press staff, so the picture I have drawn of this period is based upon impressions and information gained day by day from such close contact with Mr. Wilson and also with William B. Reid, the head clerk. Mr. Reid entered the employ of John Wilson and Son in 1865, when this establishment was still located in Boston. He was an expert compositor, and when Mr. Wilson took over the business of Welch, Bigelow & Company (the University Press) in 1879, Mr. Reid became a part of the personnel at the new location. Later he was transferred from the composition room into the counting room, so he had an opportunity to meet Mrs. Eddy earlier than I, but later than her first business conference with Mr. Wilson which I have already chronicled. In 1930 Mr. Reid prepared some "Random Recollections," which are deposited in the Archives of The Mother Church, and quotations from these "Recollections" make my picture that much the more complete. Mr. Reid records:

I can recall very distinctly just where Mrs. Eddy stood in our office — my position was nearest the door, so that I was in some contact with every person entering to do business — with her was Dr. Asa Eddy, her husband, a shortish, slim-built man. . . . Having had some of the work to do on Science and Health in the "shop," and naturally being interested in what was being said in the papers in regard to the new religion (or "cult," as most of them named it, that being the accepted title for any new movement originating around Boston), when I saw, with my own eyes, the author of what, even in those early days of the movement, was being discussed everywhere, you may be assured that I took more than one look at her, as she sat, engaged in conversation with Mr. Wilson; this proved to be needless, as it was to be my privilege to meet her many times. I have often looked at the frontispiece in Miscellaneous Writings and, mentally comparing it with other pictures, have decided, to my own satisfaction at least, that the plate there presented is the best picture of Mrs. Eddy that I have seen. She was, as I recall her, a trifle above what we call middle height, slim of figure, with brightly shining eyes, of a dark brown color, as I recall them after all these years; she wore her hair in what was then called "crimps." Her clothing was dark, and she wore a bonnet.

At this time Mrs. Eddy was living at Lynn, Massachusetts, so that proofs were delivered and returned through the mails; later I frequently called at the Massachusetts Metaphysical College on Columbus Avenue.

Not only did the completed two-volume third edition of 1881 meet all of Mrs. Eddy's expectations, but its sales fully warranted her confidence. They were not handsome volumes — there were no handsome volumes in those days — but they were well made, and the proofreading was meticulous. Volume I contained 270 pages, and Volume II 214 pages. The Cross and Crown replaced the Ark on the cover. During 1881 and 1882 three editions of one thousand copies each came off the press. In 1883 the sixth edition appeared, with the words "With a Key to the Scriptures" added to the title, the new matter consisting of a twenty-page Glossary, containing the metaphysical interpretation of Biblical terms. This wording was repeated through the fifteenth edition, when the "*a*" was dropped, and the title of the textbook became permanently established. Between this edition and 1885, nine more printings were required, each with clarifying alterations made by the author, but without resetting the type. All these fifteen editions except the first and second were issued in two-volume form.

The sale of fifteen thousand copies in ten years seems a modest record in these days of big editions, but to have any volume remain in demand for such a period, particularly when one considers the serious nature of Science and Health, was noteworthy, especially as the sales were cumulative. With each copy sold representing a convert, or a new student, it was evident that the teachings of Christian Science were taking root.

. . . .

At the time Science and Health was issued there was a distinct spirit of religious discontent throughout New England. Perhaps the clearest explanation of the cause is given by Professor Barrett Wendell, my professor in English at Harvard, in his essay on Some Neglected Characteristics of the New England Puritans:

The fatalistic creed of the Puritan fathers, while somewhat modified, still dominated the religious utterances during the last quarter of the nineteenth century. Adam in his fall, they impressed upon their congregations, exerted his will in opposition to the will of God. Therefore Adam and all his posterity merited eternal punishment. As a mark of that punishment, they lost the power of exerting this will in harmony with the will of God without losing their hereditary responsibility to Him. But God, in His infinite mercy, was pleased to mitigate His justice. Through the media of Christ certain human beings, chosen of God's pleasure, might be relieved of the just penalty of sin ancestral and personal, and received into everlasting salvation. These were the elect; none others could be saved, nor could any acts of the elect impair their salvation. (Annual Report for 1891 of American Historical Association.)

No wonder various "cults," as Mr. Reid called them, sprang up, each one offering converts its own panacea as the opportunity to escape the impending doom! Why was it that after flourishing for a time they one by one disappeared, while Christian Science continued to grow and expand its influence? In answering that question, my mind goes back to what Mrs. Eddy said to me years later, when we were discussing the production of the Bible-paper edition of Science and Health.

"It has always been my desire and expectation," she explained, "that my book should encourage more and more people to read the Bible. Through sharing the revelations of the spiritual meaning of the Bible which have come to me, Christian Scientists recognize the messages more clearly, and come to understand better what these messages mean to them."

Compare this statement with any of the escapes offered by the "cults." What one of them was based upon a foundation of living truth? Mrs. Eddy did not offer Science and Health as her panacea, except as an instrument, but rather the Bible itself. She was convinced that she had discovered the spiritually scientific meaning of the Scriptural teachings, and had received the power to present them in such a way as to enable others to understand and prove them in their own lives. Her conception of Christianity was diametrically opposed to the Puritanically created "election," and her abhorrence to this dated back to her childhood. She records in "Retrospection and Introspection" (p. 13):

I was admitted to the Congregational (Trinitarian) Church. . . . Before this step was taken, the doctrine of unconditional election, or predestination, greatly troubled me; for I was unwilling to be saved, if my brothers and sisters were to be numbered among those who were doomed to perpetual banishment from God.

She preached the theory that each individual was master of himself, and that by applying the newly understood truths contained in the Bible, each one was limited in what he could make of himself only by the extent to which he had absorbed these truths. She preached hope as against despair, joy as against sorrow. The Bible was her text; Science and Health was her textbook.

During all this period John Wilson had kept this particular order under his personal eye, and he took an unusual pride in the growing success which came to the book and to its author. He saw Mrs. Eddy frequently, and their friendship ripened. It was he who suggested to her the idea of arranging with one of his proofreaders, the Rev. James Henry Wiggin, to relieve her as she carried on her triple task of concentrating her thoughts on the all-important revision of her textbook, while teaching her classes in the Massachusetts Metaphysical College in Boston and serving as Pastor of her Church. Mr. Wiggin was an ex-Unitarian minister, highly educated, and had already demonstrated his constructive interest while preceding editions had been going through the Press. Acting on Mr. Wilson's suggestion, Mrs. Eddy engaged him specifically as literary advisor.

By this time the revision and additions made it necessary to reset Science and Health entirely, and the sixteenth edition of 1886, expanded by much new matter, presented the book as a single volume for the first time since the second edition. Mrs. Eddy hesitated for some time whether to have one volume or two, but finally decided upon a single volume, that her book might be complete in itself. "Genesis" and "The Apocalypse" appeared for the first time in this edition. From the first through the fifteenth editions inclusive, "Genesis" had been published as a separate chapter under the heading, "Creation."

The manufacturing order appeared in Mr. Wilson's record book, already referred to, under date of September 15, 1885. This time one set of proofs went to "Mrs. Mary B. G. Eddy, Metaphysical College, Columbus Avenue, Boston," and the second set to "Reverend James Henry Wiggin, 27 Hammond Street, Boston."

It was in connection with this edition that malicious rumors arose that Mr. Wiggin had personally written or rewritten substantial portions of Mrs. Eddy's manuscript. This was before my day, but Mr. Reid, in his "Random Recollections," has this comment to make:

When it was decided that it would be economy to have the copy prepared for the printer, thus saving charges for what would have been figured as "alterations from copy," if done after the type had been set up, Mr. Wiggin was detailed to do the work (punctuation, capitalization and general smoothing out as to construction of sentences), and as he did this on his own time, the payment for these

services was made by Mrs. Eddy, we having no interest in
the matter. This was well-known to those in our office,
as well as in our proof reading department, and caused many
a smile among us when we read, from time to time, the
repeated assertion that Mr. Wiggin had written the book,
and it tickled him more than perhaps any one else to read
that he was the *author* (instead of corrector). . . . I frequently dined with Mr. Wilson and Mr. Wiggin . . . and
I can recall more than one occasion when the talk would
turn on the topics of the day (Christian Science being
then one of the leading subjects), the glee with which
Mr. Wiggin would refer to the suspicion that he was the
author (and it would be some "glee," as he had a laugh in
keeping with his size), when he would say to Mr. Wilson,
"Wouldn't it have been fine if I had, and could give you
all the printing?"

I suppose that this claim is one of the lies that does
not stay nailed, and for, perhaps, personal reasons is dragged
into the light of day from time to time; but, nevertheless
this *was* a lie!

Beyond all this, Mrs. Eddy's letters gave Mr. Wiggin
explicit instructions as to the extent she desired his
assistance. On July 30, 1885, she wrote him, "Never
change my meaning, only *bring it out.*" Again, on
June 14, 1886, "They (your corrections) are all right
in grammar and I understand you should do no more
for the proofs than to attend to that." A third letter,
written in July, 1886, instructs Mr. Wiggin, "Please
send both copy and proof to me and have no alterations
made after I return the proof to press."

During 1886–1890 editions numbering through forty-eight of Science and Health were issued from the 1886 plates, each new printing containing textual corrections in cases where the author felt she could convey her message in clearer form or simpler language. But Mrs. Eddy was not satisfied. She felt that with the growing acceptance of Christian Science, and the increasing number of her enthusiastic followers, the time had come when she should push aside every diverting effort, no matter how important it had previously appeared to her, in order to concentrate definitely and completely on the rewriting and revision of the textbook. Thus it was that the Massachusetts Metaphysical College, at the height of its prosperity, was closed in 1889, and Mrs. Eddy consecrated the next two years to her self-imposed task. Mr. Wiggin was re-engaged to act as her literary adviser, showing how little attention she had paid to the earlier malicious rumors.

The statements quoted from Mr. Reid and Mrs. Eddy's letters in regard to Mr. Wiggin's association with Science and Health should have been sufficient to quiet any later misleading statements, but malicious rumors have long lives. Even while I have been writing this narrative, the matter has cropped up as strong as ever, statements being made by eminently substantial and responsible people.

I was dining one Sunday with friends of long standing. After dinner some reference was made to a

recent essay of mine which had appeared on The Home
Forum page in *The Christian Science Monitor*, and
this turned the conversation to Christian Science. My
host, who has held high positions in the financial world,
now retired, turned to me and said, casually, "You
know, of course, that Mrs. Eddy never wrote Science
and Health."

He made the statement in such a matter-of-fact way,
and with such conviction, that I was really shocked.
"It was written by a man named James Henry Wiggin,"
he continued, "who was a proofreader on the *Boston
Globe*. Mrs. Eddy herself was not competent to write
at all. She paid him $10,000 for writing Science and
Health."

"Where did you get that amazing information?" I
inquired.

My friend named a well-known Boston lawyer
whom I also know. "Wiggin lived next door to him
in Roxbury," he explained, "and told him all about it.
But why amazing?"

The minor inconsistencies of placing Mr. Wiggin
as a proofreader at the *Boston Globe* instead of at the
University Press, and as living in Roxbury instead of
in Boston, were unimportant, but since people of such
substance and reliability still seem to have such erro-
neous ideas regarding this particular subject, I propose
to record here what I actually know myself in regard
to the fiftieth edition, which was the second occasion

when certain people tried to give Mr. Wiggin credit for authorship.

During the summer vacation of 1890, between my sophomore and junior years at Harvard, I was seeking an opportunity to make extra money to help pay my college expenses. I secured a position in the proof-reading department of the University Press, and it so happened that during the next ten weeks the resetting of what is known as the fiftieth edition of Science and Health took place. This edition also became a target for misrepresentation because of the increased number of pages. One set of proofs went to Mrs. Eddy's first publisher, William G. Nixon, the second set to Mr. Wiggin. As the galleys and pages passed through the proofreading department at the University Press, both the author's copy and the proof frequently came into my hands. This copy consisted of printed pages from the previous edition containing corrections, and manu-script copy for the new matter. It would have been impossible for any of it to be in Mr. Wiggin's hand-writing or of his authorship without having it apparent to everyone in the proofreading department.

Beyond all this, it so happened that Mr. Wiggin and Mr. A. W. Stevens, the head proofreader at the University Press, were great friends of John Wilson, the proprietor. All three were fond of old-fashioned whist, and they frequently were deprived of a game by difficulty in finding a fourth player. When Mr.

Stevens discovered that I also was fond of whist, he suggested to Mr. Wilson that he invite me to complete their table at their biweekly gatherings, which occurred at John Wilson's house while his family was at the shore. I was very glad to comply, as it brought me in closer touch with my employer.

In between the games there was frequently a discussion regarding the Science and Health proof which was going through the Press at that time, as Mr. Wilson took such a peculiarly personal interest in the book. Mr. Wiggin was a vainglorious, pompous man, with a very high opinion of his own ability. In his conversations with Mr. Wilson about the proof, he constantly spoke of the difficulty he had in trying to persuade Mrs. Eddy to accept his suggestions, and he seemed to be somewhat chagrined by that fact. At no time during the summer, or during the entire period when I knew Mr. Wiggin, was there the slightest suggestion on his part that he was entitled to any credit beyond faithful service to an author in assisting her to keep the manuscript consistent and clear in statement. This service was not only what other authors accepted but what they expected. With his peculiar characteristics, there is no question whatever that Mr. Wiggin would have claimed at least whatever credit was honestly due him.

My chance employment as proofreader at the University Press, that summer of 1890, unexpectedly turned out to be the beginning of my long association with the manufacture of Mrs. Eddy's books. When I left my position to return to college in September, Mr. Stevens, the head proofreader, offered me a permanent position in his department when I graduated. Frankly, the idea of making proofreading my lifework did not appeal to me, but I thanked him for the compliment his offer implied, and explained my ambition to become a writer. I was succeeding in putting myself through Harvard University by the proceeds of my pen, and my idea was to take my degree in June, 1892, and then to spend two years at Cambridge University, England, majoring in English and securing a D. Litt. degree. This explanation he graciously accepted, and I supposed my association with the University Press was at an end.

I had not, however, figured upon an aftermath of my whist games with John Wilson. It so happened that I completed my four-year Harvard course six months ahead of the usual schedule, and became eligible for my degree in October, 1891. When Mr. Wilson learned of this, he promptly offered me a position not in the proofreading department, but in the counting room as his assistant. Again I explained my ambition to become a writer, which statement he met by saying that the engagement might be terminated at any time I chose. Thus, with the six months' period of waiting to take my degree with my class in June, 1892, I accepted, believing that a firsthand knowledge of how books were made would be a future asset in writing them.

The order for manufacturing the fiftieth edition, in the proofreading of which I participated, is entered in John Wilson's record book under date of July 2, 1890, in the name of "Rev. M. B. G. Eddy, 62 North State Street, Concord, N. H." Again two sets of proofs, one to "Rev. James H. Wiggin, 27 Hammond Street, Boston," and the second to "Mr. W. G. Nixon, 24 Boylston Street, Boston," were requested. Mrs. Eddy's instructions are again clearly stated to Mr. Wiggin in a letter under date of June 14, 1890: "I shall request Mr. Wilson to send the proofs to you and then you to me and I to him."

This fiftieth edition is the one which first carried the marginal headings. At the head of each chapter Biblical quotations were substituted for the lines of poetry and prose previously employed, and the chapters were rearranged. Its manufacture had been completed before I entered the counting room of the University Press.

William G. Nixon was Mrs. Eddy's first publisher. He came to Boston from Pierre, South Dakota, where he had been engaged in the banking business. He first served Mrs. Eddy as publisher of *The Christian Science Journal*, and was the publisher of her books from August, 1890, to January, 1893. Prior to the appointment of Mr. Nixon, the problem of distributing the

book had been just one more of the many details
Mrs. Eddy took upon her overloaded shoulders. In the
shipping room of the University Press I found entries
showing that during the period covering the publication of the third through the forty-eighth editions, John
Wilson had issued instructions to have individual shipments from the bindery supervised far beyond the
general practice with other publishers whose volumes
were being manufactured by the Press. Thus, while
small bulk shipments were made to Mrs. Eddy in Lynn,
or to the Metaphysical College at 569 Columbus Avenue,
Boston, where she was undoubtedly assisted by her students, a considerable portion was wrapped and mailed
direct from the bindery.

This burden on Mrs. Eddy was even greater than
appears at first, as during the years she had added sev-
eral shorter titles to her publishing list. Between 1887
and 1893 there appeared in book form "Unity of
Good," "Rudimental Divine Science," "No and Yes,"
"Retrospection and Introspection," and "Christ and
Christmas." The Church Manual and "Pulpit and
Press" followed in 1895. Truly, the shelf of Mrs.
Eddy's books was assuming proportions! Now, with
Mr. Nixon installed as publisher, we assumed that the
responsibility of all this individual packaging and deliv-
ery would fall upon him.

Mr. Nixon's name appears as publisher on the title
page of the fifty-first edition of Science and Health,

and this inaugurated Mrs. Eddy's plan to have the name of her publisher replace her earlier imprints. This arrangement was carried out until 1918, when the name of The Christian Science Publishing Society was given as publisher. The present imprint, "Published by the Trustees under the Will of Mary Baker G. Eddy," was made permanent in 1922.

One of the first duties assigned me was in connection with supervising shipments in bulk from the bindery to Mr. Nixon at his Boylston Street office, and to have wrapped and packed a limited number of separate copies to be mailed out to individual addresses. It is natural that the earliest responsibilities entrusted to a young man at the outset of his business career should leave an impression far out of proportion to their importance. Anyone, with or without experience, could have handled such details, but somehow the fact that Mr. Wilson entrusted me with them made Science and Health something more personal than any volume or volumes with which I later became associated. Throughout the past half century that feeling of personal interest has been intensified. During the first few months, as I became more familiar with my routine duties, I was used as messenger boy between the University Press, the bindery, and Mr. Nixon's office as the occasion required. The telephone in those days was a comparative novelty. One was installed at the Press, but Mr. Wilson would have none of it.

During that first six months' period Mr. Wilson treated me with far more attention and consideration than any young clerk in his first job had a right to expect. I was aware of this, and was grateful for it; but I attributed his attitude to the fact that I had come into the office at his suggestion, and as a temporary measure. His only son, on whom he had depended to carry on the Wilson dynasty, had gone to South America, leaving his place to be filled during his absence.

June, 1892, came and went, leaving me with my Harvard degree and unabated anticipation for my English adventure. Mr. Wilson begged me to postpone my plans. His son had been delayed in his return; I had been of real value, and he needed me for a while longer. He was very gentle in his insistence, but this made it all the more difficult for me to persist in carrying out my plans. John Wilson was a very lovable man, and looking backwards I realize that during the period I had been with him he had made me the beneficiary of some of the affection he was deprived from bestowing upon his absent son. I did not know until much later that the "delay" he had mentioned in his son's return was in fact a flat refusal to return to the business at all.

With my acceptance of the postponement, Mr. Wilson began to add to my responsibilities and to enlarge my knowledge of the business. I remember being permitted to be present as an observer during his conference with Eugene Field regarding the manufacture of Field's "Second Book of Western Verse." This was the first celebrity I had ever seen at close range, and I was deeply impressed and interested. Then Mr. Wilson turned over to me the details associated with Mrs. Eddy's books which Mr. Reid had previously handled. Mrs. Eddy had just taken up her residence at Pleasant View, Concord, New Hampshire, so this personal service required more travel than before, and my time was of less value than Mr. Reid's.

Thus it was that one day instructions came from Mr. Wilson for me to go to Concord to discuss with Mrs. Eddy personally a matter she had previously taken up with him. Mrs. Eddy had never come to the Press during the months I had been there, but Mr. Wilson had met her frequently in Boston, at Mr. Nixon's office or at the retail bookstore of Little, Brown & Company, 254 Washington Street. The University Press did all the manufacturing for this firm at that time, and Little, Brown & Company courteously allowed Mr. Wilson to have conferences with other clients at a desk at the rear of the store.

So Mrs. Eddy was to be the second celebrity I was to know, and I found myself anticipating the opportunity keenly. I should have been prepared through Mr. Wilson's and Mr. Reid's extended conversations concerning her for the personality I was to meet, but when a name has become associated with a great move-

ment, one instinctively and unconsciously surrounds it
with unwarranted mysticism. Mrs. Eddy had made a
deep impression on Mr. Wilson. In speaking of her
he emphasized particularly her undaunted courage in
meeting and overcoming obstacles placed in her path
by disloyal and self-interested students, as well as those
who openly resented the constantly growing scope of
her work. Mrs. Eddy and Mr. Wilson had been friends
now for over ten years, and I had reason to believe
that they discussed personal problems with each other
beyond what anyone outside could know. Perhaps
because of this the orders for Mrs. Eddy's books came
to be recognized by all of us at the Press as in a preferred class, receiving detailed attention throughout
the plant far beyond their comparative commercial
value from a business point of view.

Calvin A. Frye, Mrs. Eddy's secretary, met me at
the Concord railroad station in the carriage which
became so familiar to those who knew Mrs. Eddy at
that time, and drove me to Pleasant View, the unpretentious but lovely estate Mrs. Eddy had so recently
acquired. Here I was shown into the study, and after
a brief wait a slight, unassuming woman entered the
room, giving me a smiling welcome which placed me
completely at my ease. She was not the type I had
expected her to be at all. The force of character that I
had associated with the woman as Mr. Wilson described
her was to be discovered later through the promptness

and finality of her decisions rather than by any personal aggressiveness of manner or obvious self-consciousness. She was seventy-one years old at that time, but seemed much younger. As she greeted me, I was conscious of a motherly approach which was entirely unexpected. This became clearer to me after her first words of welcome.

"So you are the young man who has been helping my friend John Wilson during his son's absence," she said. "He has told me a great deal about you. Please sit down. I am glad to know you."

This was the first inkling I had that Mr. Wilson had seen fit to make me the subject of any of his conversations with Mrs. Eddy, but as time went on I came to understand the reason. During these ten years she had found him unswervingly loyal and staunch not only in their business dealings but as a friend. He had been passing through a period of deep unhappiness because of his son's defection; she, during the same time, was experiencing disillusionment concerning her adopted son, Dr. E. J. Foster-Eddy. I could, of course, have known nothing of these things at that time, but later Mr. Wilson spoke quite freely of the comfort she had given him during that trial by fire. This confidence could not have been one-sided. Her interest in me at the beginning was due to her belief that I was an essential piece to be fitted into her friend's design for living, to repair a break that had occurred. If she, as John

Wilson's friend, could help him to accomplish this, she intended to do so. That was her idea of what friendship meant.

After a few moments of general conversation we turned to the proof sheets I had brought with me, and the questions Mr. Wilson had wished settled were answered with promptness and directness. At first, one might have been deceived by her quiet manner into thinking that she was easily influenced. There was no suggestion to which she did not hold herself open. If she approved, she accepted it promptly; if it did not appeal, she dismissed it with a graciousness that left no mark — but it was settled once and for all. There was no wavering and no uncertainty. With my business completed, I naturally rose to leave, but she motioned me to resume my seat.

"Don't go yet," she said graciously. "Your train doesn't leave for three quarters of an hour. I want to understand better why my friend is so eager to keep you with him."

"Mr. Wilson has been very kind to me," I explained, "and I'm glad to learn from what he has told you that I have been of some help to him." And then, without my realizing it, during the next quarter hour Mrs. Eddy quietly drew from me a full statement of my boyish hopes and aspirations. It proved a very easy task to confide in Mrs. Eddy! When I left Pleasant View that day I felt as if I had known her all my life. On the train going back to Boston I found myself wondering why she should have shown such interest as to encourage me to take her time, which even then I knew to be so heavily pre-empted.

With our personal relations so happily established at our very first meeting, it was natural that they should develop progressively during the following years. I had found myself absolutely unable to break away from Mr. Wilson, and I was none too happy about it. There was no question that he needed me — he was feeling the effect of his advancing years, and affairs were not going well between him and his partner. It was unthinkable that I should add to his unhappiness by deserting him. During this period I came more and more in touch with Mr. Nixon, and with his successor, Dr. E. J. Foster-Eddy; but from time to time I was called to Pleasant View. From casual remarks I was by this time quite aware that Mrs. Eddy and Mr. Wilson, during their meetings in Boston, discussed personal matters beyond the routine of the business, so I was not wholly unprepared, during one of our conferences in the study, to have her say:

"I can't understand why you are not interested in becoming John Wilson's successor at the University Press. That seems to me to be a future to which any young man might look forward."

Mrs. Eddy was right. It was a wonderful opportunity to become the head of the oldest printing establishment in British North America, the lineal descendant of the Press which produced the Bay Psalm Book and John Eliot's Indian Bible. But somehow the idea did not appeal to me. I had become deeply interested in my study of the work of the early master printers, and as a result of my study I had come to feel strongly that in America printers were permitting their concentration upon mechanical excellence to crowd out the art that made of the fifteenth-century typographical masterpieces examples which have never been surpassed. The universal practice of the 1890's was to build a book as a series of contracts, instead of treating it architecturally as the complete product of a single mind. No emphasis seemed to be laid on the co-ordination of the type face, the arrangement of the printed page, the paper, the margins, and the binding which was demanded if a book was to serve as a harmonious vehicle for the thought the author wished to convey to his reader.

All this I explained to Mrs. Eddy, and I found her an interested listener. Still she saw nothing in what I said to warrant my objections. When I closed my youthful academic presentation by adding, "I want to devote myself to something in which there is beauty," she smiled and said quietly:

"Have you never realized that if a man has beauty in himself, he can put beauty into anything? Of course you are right in your conception of the ideal book, but it seems to me that what Mr. Wilson has in mind for you would give you the most wonderful opportunity in the world to put your ideas into action."

There was no answer to that statement, and what Mrs. Eddy said that day had much to do with the fact that I have spent my entire life in the Kingdom of Books.

During the three years 1892–1895 most of my visits to Pleasant View were to straighten out complications which arose from the inefficiency of Mrs. Eddy's first two publishers. It seemed impossible for this indefatigable woman to relieve herself of the business details, so that she might devote her time to that part of her work which she alone could do. And the business details were demanding and essential to supply the funds to make the continuation of her efforts possible. It had been evident from the first that Mr. Nixon's earlier training as a banker in South Dakota had not fitted him to play the role of publisher. Everything that passed through his hands moved slowly, with no idea of co-ordinating the proofs, the paper, the binding orders essential to getting out each new edition, with Mrs. Eddy's latest clarifications, in time to keep copies in stock. His association with the resetting of the fiftieth edition slowed the work down, his set of proofs was returned tardily, and he seemed to resent the pressure that had to be put upon him in order to meet Mrs. Eddy's wishes in producing the finished books.

When Mrs. Eddy removed Mr. Nixon from his position as publisher in January, 1893, we at the University Press were prepared to give his successor, Dr. E. J. Foster-Eddy, a graduate of Hahnemann Medical College, Philadelphia, a cordial welcome. But again a disappointment. I shall never forget the first time I saw him. He arrived at the University Press in a cab, which he had wait for him. This in itself was sensational, for our other clients, including Mrs. Eddy, made use of the less luxurious horsecars from Scollay Square. He was immaculately dressed, the climax being his magnificent fur-lined coat, fur cap, and the stunning diamond in his shirtfront. We found in him an agreeable personality, with a gratifying willingness to accept suggestions and make promises to co-operate; but there it stopped. Over and over again we had to refer details direct to Mrs. Eddy because Dr. Foster-Eddy was not at his office, and could not be located for days at a time. During the six years when Mr. Nixon and Dr. Foster-Eddy served, 61,000 copies of Science and Health had been manufactured, to say nothing of the other titles, which emphasized the accompanying detail. Acting on Mr. Wilson's instructions, I threw myself into the breach wherever possible, but the responsibility which Mrs. Eddy still had to assume personally was unfortunate.

Other matters at the University Press were moving badly. Mrs. Eddy's books represented but a single account in a large manufacturing business. As a result of Mr. Wilson's high personal and professional standards, the volume of work steadily increased, requiring enlarged facilities and increased personnel. The business horizon looked particularly bright in 1894, but, unknown to Mr. Wilson, his partner for some time had so mismanaged the financial affairs that the whole business structure had become impaired, and the Press faced bankruptcy. As the finances had been entirely in this partner's hands, and as Mr. Wilson had implicit confidence in his ability, the precarious situation had remained undiscovered almost until the crash came.

And when it came, John Wilson received a shock from which he never recovered. I doubt if he once thought of the financial loss — he felt his honor to be involved. His many friends rallied around him, showing in every way that they absolved him from personal responsibility, but nothing relieved his sense of shame and consequent despondency. A touching example of loyalty was when a group of the old employees came to Mr. Wilson's office with bankbooks in their hands, placing their meager savings at his disposal.

One of the first injunctions he placed upon me was to see Mrs. Eddy personally, and to explain everything to her. "This may affect the manufacture of her books," he said; "but particularly I want her to know that this

wretched affair is not of my doing. I could not bear
to lose her respect and her friendship."

This was the unhappiest and yet the most revealing
visit I ever made to Pleasant View. Mrs. Eddy had
learned of the assignment through the daily press, but
was eager to know the inside facts. As Mr. Wilson
had said, this disaster to the University Press might
affect the manufacture of her books, but her concern
was wholly in its effect on her friend. After a detailed
account of all that had led up to the assignment, and
an explanation of the probable future trend of affairs,
her earliest reaction interested me.

"We must think of John Wilson first, and the
business afterwards," she said. "Does he need immediate cash?" This was a question I could not answer.
"Of course he does," she answered her own question.
"I shall send him a check by you. And especially a
message. Tell him to be of good cheer. What he has
given of himself to others all these years must now
return to him a thousandfold."

When I left Pleasant View she handed me an enve-
lope containing her check for a substantial amount.
This I delivered to Mr. Wilson with her message. The
obvious pleasure he derived from her sympathy, and
the motive which prompted her tangible expression of
it, confirmed my belief that their friendship was very
deeply rooted.

The untangling of the mixed affairs at the Uni-

versity Press during the next two years has no place
in this narrative except as it affects Mrs. Eddy and the
printing of her books. A creditors' committee took
temporary charge of the business, and during the
reorganization the Press was continued as a going concern with William B. Reid, Mr. Wilson's head clerk,
acting as Receiver. In due course new capital was
forthcoming; a Massachusetts corporation was formed,
Mr. Wilson being allotted 45 per cent of the stock,
the new capital taking over 55 per cent and the control.
A new building was projected and built on the bank of
the Charles River, not far from the old location, and by
1896 all was reorganized and the business had started
out on a new era. The old clients remained loyal and
co-operative, and on the surface all seemed serene.

The real facts, however, did not confirm this. Mr.
Wilson became president of the newly formed corporation, and made a brave effort to fit into the picture;
but after having been the autocrat of what he considered his own business for so many years, he found
it impossible to accept the fact that his actions now
were subject to whatever policy the board of directors
might indicate. To complicate matters, Mr. Wilson's
wandering son took this moment to return from his
unsuccessful challenge of the world, and his great-
hearted father insisted on forcing him into the office
staff where he did not fit by nature, experience, or
inclination. The shock Mr. Wilson had sustained

greatly impaired his initiative and judgment, and Mr. Reid and I, in addition to our other duties, had to assume the responsibility of smoothing out countless differences of opinion between him and the new officers of the corporation. The fact that they knew nothing of the technical side of bookmaking made Mr. Wilson resentful of what he considered their interference in his running of the business.

All this added to my own desire to break away, and at long last gratify my dream of authorship which had been frustrated so many times, but everything that happened at the Press seemed to forge an additional link to the chain. During this period Mrs. Eddy had been trying to bring out an edition of Science and Health printed on Bible paper, and Mr. Wilson's half-hearted efforts had not proved successful. This in itself indicated the change that had come over her old friend, and she was deeply concerned, especially when she learned from me that he had become a virtual recluse, performing his routine duties perfunctorily at his desk, but instructing me to keep up the personal contacts with customers, which formerly gave him so much pleasure. He considered himself a discredited and humiliated man.

Beyond the natural sympathy Mrs. Eddy felt and expressed for Mr. Wilson, she was bound also to feel concern over what effect the confused situation might have upon the production of her books. I did not know it at the time, but she had in mind a new and important volume embracing her writings during the past few years. The handling of the old titles at the Press had been virtually in my hands for years through Mr. Wilson's instructions. Mrs. Eddy needed to know who would carry on this business if I insisted on leaving. The trust she put in me at this point was another link in the chain, and her advice to me had a strong influence in keeping me at my post until the climax came and a final decision had to be made.

This climax was reached early in 1897. The impossibility of Mr. Wilson continuing became more and more apparent to everyone, including himself. His first move was to offer me the opportunity to buy his stock, but that idea seemed absolutely absurd, first because Mr. Reid seemed to be his logical successor, and, second, because I was without financial background.

"I have discussed the matter with Mr. Reid," Mr. Wilson told me, "and he wants you to take my place. Reid is a fine fellow, but he has come up from the case, and has had no experience in assuming responsibility. He doesn't know the customers as you do. Reid would be a great help to you, but he could never sit in my chair."

What Mr. Wilson said was true. During the receivership, while Mr. Reid was acting head of the business, he was constantly referring important matters to me for final decision. But even so I protested.

"I have always wanted you to carry the torch," John Wilson continued, "ever since I knew that my own son could not be my successor. You are young, your experience is insufficient, but you know the business as a whole better than anyone else here. I hope — "

I interrupted to prevent him from putting that hope into words. He was making it very hard for me.

"What you have just said," I told him, "is ample reason for my not considering the matter seriously. First of all, I have stayed on here for five years because you needed me. Now you are leaving, and the business without you doesn't interest me. As to the capital, I realize my youth and inexperience better than anyone else, and I would never ask a friend to take financial risk on me."

Mr. Wilson was still insistent. "Then I will ask you one more thing. Before you make your final decision, talk the matter over with Joe Phinney and Mrs. Eddy. Both of these dear friends know how I feel, and they also know your relations with the business."

Joseph W. Phinney, to whom John Wilson referred, was president of the American Type Founders Company in Boston, and had been chairman of the creditors' committee. I repeated to him even more forcibly my absolute unwillingness to seek financial support from my friends, and he seemed sympathetic to my reaction rather than to John Wilson's suggestion. He simply asked me to take no definite action one way or the other without seeing him again. I defaulted in carrying out Mr. Wilson's suggestion to talk the matter over with Mrs. Eddy, feeling that she had too many problems of her own without adding mine, which I felt would be an unwarranted intrusion. Within a week Mr. Phinney sent for me and announced that friends of mine and of the business, absolutely unsolicited by me, and without my knowledge, had offered to advance the capital necessary for me to purchase John Wilson's stock, taking certificates of the new corporation as collateral. He handed me a slip of paper containing the names of these friends, and among them was that of Mary Baker G. Eddy.

Who could still advance objections against such a vote of confidence! But it was Mrs. Eddy's gracious act of kindness that touched me most. I made a special trip to Pleasant View to thank her not only for the tangible evidence of her approval, but for the encouragement it gave me. She accepted my protestations lightly. "This is a business transaction," she said simply. "I want my books to continue to be manufactured the way they always have been, and your presence at the head of the University Press will insure just that."

I like to think that, during the years which followed, her expectation has been fulfilled.

PART II

Mrs. Eddy and the Author
1897 - 1910

Mrs. Eddy and the Author
1897 - 1910

JOHN WILSON left the University Press in March, 1897, and sailed with his son for a long vacation in South America. Of course we all knew, as he did himself, that he would never return to his desk again, and the parting was difficult. He tried to assume an outward semblance of relief, but Mr. Wilson was no actor, and his brave efforts were pathetic. While waiting with him for the train to leave the station to take him to New York, he loaded me down with instructions, mostly trivial, and messages to his friends. Among them was one for Mrs. Eddy:

"Make her understand," he begged, "why I could not see her. I was ashamed. She has done so much for me. Take her my thanks and gratitude."

Immediately after Mr. Wilson's departure, the directors of the University Press elected me vice president and general manager, and the new era had begun. By this time also a new era had begun for Mrs. Eddy's manufacturing, which corrected the disorganization and lack of discipline which had existed for too long a time in the office of her publisher, Dr. E. J. Foster-Eddy. During the period required for the reorganization of the University Press, conferences had been required between Mrs. Eddy and myself which would have been wholly unnecessary, except for the chaos which existed in Dr. Foster-Eddy's office. Mrs. Eddy realized this, and, while she said little, she appreciated that, with the added responsibilities which fell on me as a result of the business collapse, these unnecessary details were burdensome. When, in July, 1896, she announced to me that she had dismissed Dr. Foster-Eddy and appointed Joseph Armstrong as her publisher, the news was received with a sigh of relief and with optimistic expectations.

Mr. Armstrong was a banker, as Mr. Nixon had been, but was quite a different type of man. He had come to Boston from Kansas three years earlier to become Manager of The Christian Science Publishing Society. In March of that same year he was appointed to The Christian Science Board of Directors.

"Mr. Armstrong is not familiar with bookmaking," Mrs. Eddy said to me when she announced his appointment, "but he is a good businessman. You will have to advise him to a certain extent, and you are still to refer any problem to me that you may think necessary."

"Over his head?" I inquired rather anxiously, foreseeing possible complications. I realized at once that I had said the wrong thing.

Mrs. Eddy stiffened for a moment as she answered, with quiet dignity, "It will be over no one's head;

Mr. Armstrong is engaged to assist me and to carry out my instructions. I am the head."

This incident is recorded as it impressed upon me the constantly recurring fact that the relief which came to this indefatigable woman from the lifting of the burden of comparatively unimportant but essential details did not remove her insistence to continue her personal responsibility. She was content to permit others to gather together the salient facts, and to reduce them to such a point that she could visualize all the angles, but the final decision must be hers. The speed with which she absorbed these facts, and the directness of her vision as expressed in her decisions, presented an extraordinary exhibition of her inherent and instinctive business foresight.

Thus it was that, throughout Mr. Armstrong's regime, the routine was for me to advise with the publisher concerning the matter under discussion, but to await formal decision from Mrs. Eddy herself. And these written decisions, curiously enough in view of the unusual informality of our personal conferences, were exceedingly formal, the address invariably being "My dear Sir" and the signature "Very respectfully, Mary Baker G. Eddy."

During the regime of Mr. Armstrong, the office of publisher really began to function for the first time. His imprint first appears on the one hundred and eleventh edition, and extended into 1907, by which date the custom of numbering the editions had been discontinued. We at the Press were relieved from all responsibility on shipping beyond delivery in bulk to Mr. Armstrong's office. The manufacturing details by this time had settled themselves into a routine, which allowed Mrs. Eddy more quiet and peace as she devoted herself tirelessly to the rewriting and revision of what she intended to be the final and completely rounded-out presentation of her message to the world.

The earliest matter of major importance which I had to take up with Mrs. Eddy after I assumed charge of the University Press was that of printing Science and Health on Bible paper. Mrs. Eddy had first broached the subject in 1893, much to John Wilson's embarrassment. Printing on Bible paper in the 1890's was rarely called for, and in fact had never been attempted at the University Press. More than this, John Wilson did not adapt himself readily to any departure from the regular routine of the printing business, of which he was recognized as past master. In the present instance he placed upon me the responsibility of discussing the matter with Mrs. Eddy at Pleasant View.

"Talk it over with her frankly," he instructed me in his rare Scottish accent. "We mustn't seem unwilling to do anything she asks, but to print on Bible paper means a deal of trouble for all concerned."

She listened patiently to my presentation of Mr. Wilson's message. Then, with her characteristic insistence upon detail, she asked me just why Mr. Wilson felt the undertaking would be troublesome. I was prepared for this question, as I had spent some time answering it to myself. To make forms of type ready to print on this thin paper required a technique quite different from that ordinarily employed for printing upon heavier paper, and the feeding of these thin sheets into the press twice, to print on both sides, and have the pages register, was no mean undertaking. To secure even partially successful results, the press would have to be run much more slowly, and, most important of all, where could Bible paper be secured in America?

After I had presented my dissertation as clearly as I could, Mrs. Eddy took over the conversation. "I am glad to know the problems," she said, "but I see nothing in them that cannot be overcome. What printers have done in England printers can do here. I am going to tell you why I wish Science and Health to be printed on Bible paper. When you explain this to Mr. Wilson, I am sure he will be eager to co-operate."

Then she made the following statement, which I wrote out to make sure that her message would be correctly delivered. During the years I have had many opportunities to quote it in conversations with persons unfriendly to Christian Science, who have asserted that Mrs. Eddy regarded Science and Health as a substitute rather than as an interpreter of the Bible.

"It has always been my desire and expectation," she

said, "that my book should encourage more and more people to read the Bible. Through sharing the revelation of the spiritual meaning of the Bible which has come to me, Christian Scientists recognize the messages more clearly, and understand better what these messages mean to them. Many have suggested the desirability of having the Bible and Science and Health more similar in physical appearance as an aid in using them together. It would gratify them very much to be able to secure copies of Science and Health on similar paper, and it would gratify me very much to gratify them."

Needless to say, Mr. Wilson responded fully and promptly. In due time the first lot of paper was received from Dr. Foster-Eddy, and was run through the press in April, 1893, as the seventy-fifth edition of Science and Health, but the stock supplied was really not Bible paper at all, completely lacking its peculiar characteristics. Instead, it was a thinner sheet of text paper on which the type showed to much poorer advantage than in the regular edition. Mrs. Eddy accepted this and made no comment. In November of that same year, the eightieth edition was printed on this same thin paper, and in April, 1894, two hundred and forty copies of the eighty-second edition were issued on this stock. None of these printings was satisfactory to Mr. Wilson or to Mrs. Eddy.

In 1894, however, the problem took a step toward being solved. Four years previously, Edward P. Bates, an ardent Christian Scientist who later became a Director, had his attention called to a copy of the Oxford Bible, printed on a paper quite different from anything he had ever before seen. On inquiry, the Oxford University Press people told him its history.

In 1841, a graduate of Oxford, returning home from China, brought with him a small quantity of remarkably thin paper, which was stronger and more opaque for its substance than any paper at that time manufactured in Europe. This specimen was presented as a curiosity to the Oxford University Press, Thomas Combe then being University Printer, and the paper was used to print twenty-four copies of a tiny Bible, bearing the date 1842. These were not offered for sale, but were presented to Queen Victoria and to other personages. Mr. Combe tried to trace this paper to its source but failed. He even asked the aid of the Prime Minister, Mr. Gladstone. Paper was obtained from all quarters, but, though the samples were equally thin and tough, they did not possess the opacity of the Chinese specimen, and could not be printed on both sides.

Many years passed, and this little piece of Chinese paper was almost forgotten, but in 1874 Arthur E. Miles brought a copy of the little Bible to Henry Frowde, who was then University Printer, and suggested that experiments be made at the Wolvercote Mills to reproduce it. After years of experimentation, success was achieved, and a facsimile of the tiny Bible printed in

1842 was produced. The demand for this was so great that a quarter of a million copies were sold. The process of making the paper has always been kept a closely guarded secret, and no employee is familiar with more than one stage of the manufacture.

Mr. Bates was deeply impressed. Knowing of Mrs. Eddy's efforts to produce copies of Science and Health on Bible paper, he made a strenuous effort to purchase some of this product, but his request was refused by the Oxford American representative in a statement that Oxford India paper was used only in the printing of Bibles and Prayer Books. The question was then referred to the headquarters of the Oxford University Press in England, and the answer was returned that none of the paper was for sale. The matter was not dropped. The request was renewed, and four years later enough of the paper was purchased to print fifty copies of the textbook. Thus in May, 1894, the records of the University Press show, an experimental run was made as a part of the eighty-fourth edition.

Now the trouble for Mr. Wilson and the pressman had really begun! The earliest paper supplied in 1893, while thin, possessed more body than the genuine Bible paper sheet, and this new kind of paper required a make-ready quite apart from that adapted to any other paper stock. In his "Random Recollections," William B. Reid, head clerk at the University Press, records, "How many times I have climbed the two long steep flights of stairs leading to their [Dudley & Hodge's] bindery, and have come away with a handful of sheets 'out of register' . . . of no use in these books, to be made up in the next run."

The fifty copies which constituted the experimental run showed varying degrees of register and color. While recognizing the imperfections, Mrs. Eddy felt assured that with the discovery of the right paper, the printing defects could be overcome. The Oxford University Press by this time had been made to realize how much the circulation of Science and Health was doing to stimulate the demand for Bibles. They reversed their earlier decision, and finally entered into arrangements with The Christian Science Publishing Society to supply them, and them alone, with this Oxford India paper. The University Press records show that it was employed on the 85th, 88th, and 91st editions in 1894, the 92nd, 97th, 99th, and 100th editions in 1895, and in the 106th, 109th, and 111th editions in 1896. This arrangement for Oxford paper held firm down to the declaration of World War II in 1939. During that war the Oxford Mills were commandeered for war work, and had to decline orders. Fortunately, in anticipation of some complication, experiments which had taken place during the preceding five years had produced an American Bible paper of comparable quality.

During the period 1894–1896 each progressive edition showed an improvement over the one which preceded it, but the quality of the presswork failed to approach that of the Oxford Bibles printed in England, and the waste in the paper because of imperfect sheets was terrific. With rare understanding and consideration, Mrs. Eddy had refrained from uttering a word of criticism which might add to Mr. Wilson's unhappiness caused by the failure of the University Press, and the complications in the reorganization. She knew that he was doing his best, and at that time there was probably no printer in America who could have done better. Now that Mr. Wilson had left the Press, and the new era had begun, she wanted to know what could be done to improve the situation. Hence my summons to a personal conference. I had studied the situation thoroughly, and this was what I found.

In 1896, the American Bible Society of New York was publishing Bibles in various styles, printing its own editions in the Bible House at Astor Place. These were probably the best American printed Bibles on the market, but they did not compare with those printed in England by the Oxford University Press and the Cambridge University Press. James Pott and Company distributed Bibles printed in England by Samuel Bagster and Sons. The Oxford University Press established its New York branch in the fall of that year, and planned to print Bibles and other publications in New York. Other publishers of lesser reputation issued Bibles in various forms.

In response to Mrs. Eddy's inquiry as to procedure, I proposed that I spend some days in New York, together with the foreman of the University Press cylinder pressroom, to make an exhaustive study of the technique of Bible-paper printing as it was practiced in America at the time, with a special effort to discover what made the English production better than our own. This plan appealed to Mrs. Eddy, and I put it into operation at once. I found the New York publishers interested and co-operative. During the years which followed we shared experiments. An experienced Bible-paper pressman was secured from England and installed at the University Press in Cambridge, Massachusetts. From that point the quality of the presswork on Science and Health, and the other titles which followed it, steadily improved.

Mrs. Eddy's volumes in this thin, light form attracted attention beyond the Christian Scientists, who welcomed them. Publishers in general found titles on their trade lists which definitely called for this treatment. American paper mills were stimulated by the demand to experiment in producing paper along the lines of the Oxford Bible. American printers prepared themselves to handle these thin sheets successfully. American manufacturers of printing machinery co-operated with improved presses and new ingenious contrivances to overcome the recognized difficulties. In 1910 the eleventh edition of the Encyclopædia Britannica was issued on Bible paper supplied by an American mill, and Bible-paper printing had become a definite part of the routine in American book manufacture.

When I stand, as I often do, beside one of the great presses from which sheets of Science and Health are issuing with ease and accuracy—sixty-four pages at a time instead of sixteen as in the old days, automatic gadgets handling every detail with greater precision than could the human hand — and realize that today no country can surpass the quality of Bible-paper press-work as executed in America, my mind goes back to those early days of anxious experiment. I recall the patient understanding with which Mrs. Eddy accepted the shortcomings, and the encouragement she gave by her unwavering confidence that the difficulties could be overcome. When the history of American printing is written, she should be given high credit for her contribution to the development of this phase of the printing art.

During this same year of 1897 the "Kelmscott Chaucer," designed and printed by William Morris in England, made its completed appearance in America. Morris was an Oxford man, originally intending to enter the Church, but a vacation trip through the Cathedral towns of France placed him so heavily under the Gothic influence that he decided to take up architecture; then Rossetti's work affected him and he began to study painting, at which he was never successful, although

he showed some ability as an illuminator of books.
From this he turned toward decoration and designing
— rugs, wallpaper, stained glass. One after another he
tested out various *media* to convey a message he felt
within him, and at last settled upon the Book.

The first time one of these volumes came into my
hands my mind went instantly back to that early conference with Mrs. Eddy at Pleasant View, when she
had said, "If a man has beauty in himself he can put
beauty into anything." So, on one of my visits, I took
a copy of the "Kelmscott Chaucer" with me. When
our business conference was ended, I opened the package, and handed the volume to Mrs. Eddy with the
comment,

"Here, I believe, is an example which illustrates what
you said to me years ago about putting beauty into
books."

She looked at me thoughtfully for a moment, and
then began to turn the various pages of the volume on
the table. She was deeply interested, but before she
spoke I continued,

"Here is a man who has beauty in himself, and he
has put that beauty into the books he makes."

She looked up smiling. "Yes," she said, "this is what
I meant, and I am interested to see that you recognize it."

Then I added, "If this man Morris can transform
printing from a trade into an art, he is certainly worth
studying."

"Yes," Mrs. Eddy again assented promptly, "well worth studying, but not with the idea of copying. William Morris has beauty in himself, but he uses a strange method of expressing it. I don't like the type because it is not legible, but some people might consider it beautiful. The decoration is beautiful in itself, but Morris has not realized the importance of keeping these two beautiful things distinct, and has therefore failed in his effort to convey the beauty of the text. The decoration overshadows and confuses the understanding of the other parts of the picture."

Frankly, I was surprised and disappointed. The "Kelmscott Chaucer" seemed to me to demonstrate exactly what Mrs. Eddy had said to me that day now so long past. Surely, what William Morris had been seeking for, as he experimented in various undertakings, was to express a beauty that he had within him. I was forced to admit that his type was not particularly legible, but to me it was beautiful. Perhaps his printed page *was* overloaded with type and decoration, but to me the combination was superlatively beautiful.

Mrs. Eddy could not fail to see my reaction. She smiled and said: "Don't make the mistake that William Morris has made of looking at this through your eyes instead of through your mind. That is what has kept him shifting from one frustration to another. Everything he has done shows the same overloading and overelaboration, even his efforts to reorganize society."

She was quite right. There is no question that Morris felt keenly the contrast between the beauty in nature and the ugliness in the products of human labor, but he made the mistake of considering himself the High Priest in the Religion of Beauty, ordained to force the people to furnish and decorate their homes with things *he* thought beautiful. It apparently never occurred to him that perhaps the workingman might have some idea of his own as to what was an improvement in his surroundings, and how it should be obtained.

At this moment when Mrs. Eddy was criticizing the "Kelmscott Chaucer," the whole world was greeting it not only with admiration but with incredulity. Was it really possible to introduce such art, such beauty into a printed book? The only exception I found to the general acclaim was on the part of my old professor in art at Harvard University, Charles Eliot Norton. He was even more severe than Mrs. Eddy. "Printing," he declared, "has so seldom been practiced as a Fine Art that there is the more reason for regret when an artist of such force as Morris gives to it a wrong direction."

Then gradually came a reaction among booklovers and critics. In 1900 Thomas James Cobden-Sanderson wrote in his "Ideal Book":

The Book Beautiful is a composite thing made up of many parts, and may be made beautiful by the beauty of each of its parts in subordination to the whole which collectively they constitute; or it may be made beautiful by the supreme beauty of one or more of its parts, all the other parts subordinating or even effacing themselves for the sake of this one or more. On the other hand, each contributory craft may usurp the functions of the rest and of the whole, and growing beautiful beyond all bounds ruin for its own the common cause.

The "Kelmscott Chaucer" is not mentioned by name, but everyone recognized Cobden-Sanderson's reference as expressing the common consensus of opinion. What he said was exactly what I am sure Mrs. Eddy had in mind, but it is significant that the world required four years to reach this conclusion. Professor Norton had devoted his life to a study of art, so it was perhaps natural that he should have so promptly recognized Morris' shortcomings. Mrs. Eddy had received no such training, yet she had sensed these weaknesses practically at first glance. It was an amazing exhibition of apperception.

During this same period I had much to think of besides the details of any single manufacturing problem. The work of reorganization and of adjusting the new and heavy responsibilities occupied me fully. My dream of going to Cambridge University was shattered, but I found the pressing business problems quite sufficient to hold my interest, particularly after my adventure with the Morris volumes, and the inspiration that came with the knowledge of what could be done in transforming a trade into an art. I had come to agree wholly

with Mrs. Eddy's prompt recognition of what seemed
to be the major defect in Morris' work. By studying
what lay behind his design, and avoiding the mistake
of copying, as Mrs. Eddy had cautioned, I gained a
broader viewpoint on the whole subject of making
books. Zealous printers, who were not so fortunate as
I in receiving Mrs. Eddy's warning, produced com-
binations of type and decoration which were literally
monstrosities, and gave American bookmaking a set-
back which required years to overcome. George Ber-
nard Shaw, in a letter to me dated as late as July 13,
1905, writes:

> English printers regard an American printer as a mon-
> ster, thanks to your Roycroft shops, sham Kelmscotts, and
> other horrors; but if you approach them as a repentant
> prodigal, really desirous of spreading the light in Darkest
> America, you can find out from them all that there is to
> be found out about printing in the world.

How well I remember Mrs. Eddy's amusement as
we read this letter together!

Although the quality of the books issued from the
University Press at this point compared favorably with
that of any other plant, I was still dissatisfied; but, as I
have already recorded, I had become satisfied in my
own mind as to what was wrong with American
bookmaking: it was a contracting rather than a manufacturing business. A book was conceived and made

by the combined efforts of the publisher, the manufacturing man, the artist, the decorator, the paper mill's agent, and, last of all, the printer and the binder. This was not the way the old-time printers had planned their books. With all their mechanical limitations, they had followed architectural lines kept consistent and harmonious because controlled by a single mind, while the finished volumes of the 1890's were a composite production of many minds, with no architectural plan. No wonder that the volumes manufactured, even in the most famous presses, failed to compare with those produced in Venice by Jenson and Aldus four centuries earlier!

Thus I came to a definite conclusion that I would follow the example of the early master printers insofar as this could be done amidst modern conditions. My publisher friends became slowly convinced by my contention that if a printer properly fulfilled his function, he must know how to express his client's mental conception of the physical attributes of a prospective volume in terms of type, paper, presswork, and binding better than the client could do it himself.

What I wanted to do was to build low-cost volumes upon the same principles as de luxe editions, eliminating the expensive materials but retaining the harmony and consistency that come from designing a book from an architectural standpoint. It adds nothing to the expense to select a type that properly expresses the thought which the author wishes to convey, or to have the presses touch the letters into the paper in such a way as to become a part of it, without that heavy impression which makes the reverse side appear like an example of Braille; or to find a machine-made paper, soft to the feel and grateful to the eye, on which the page can be placed with well-considered margins; or to use illustrations or decorations, if warranted at all, in such a way as to assist the imagination of the reader rather than to divert him from the text; or to plan a title page which, like the door to a house, invites the reader to open it and enter, its type lines being carefully balanced with the blank; or to bind, even in cloth, with trig squares, and with design or lettering in keeping with the printing inside.

By degrees the publishers began to realize that this could be done, and, when once established, the idea of treating and making a book as a manufacturing problem instead of as a series of contracts with different concerns, no one of which knew what the others were doing, found favor. The authors also preferred it, as their literary children now went forth to the world in more becoming dress.

This whole conception of introducing beauty into low-cost books and gaining the approval of the publishers to its adoption required several years, and during all this period Mrs. Eddy encouraged me to keep her in touch with its unfolding. From the beginning it had her unqualified support. The very first time I mentioned the idea to her, in between discussions of her own publishing problems, she exclaimed:

"But that is the way Science and Health has always been produced — Mr. Wilson originally determined all the materials that went into the book, and since Mr. Wilson you have supervised everything and maintained the consistency."

"Yes," I assented, "and that is why Science and Health has always been an outstanding example of quality bookmaking. In this case it was a happy accident that forced us to do the natural, which proved to be the right thing. Mr. Wilson knew instinctively what type to use, and as there was no one else to select the paper, he used his own judgment in deciding on the quality and grade he knew from the experience of a printer would show the type to the best advantage, and making the margins correct by established precedents."

I made a point of limiting myself in these discussions, as I was having opportunity to witness more and more closely the tremendous demand upon Mrs. Eddy's time, and on one occasion I voiced my apprehension lest I was assuming too much in the matter of her interest. She replied, in that kindly but definitive way of hers when occasion seemed to demand it:

"You must not feel that. If I could not spare the time I would have told you. You are giving, I am receiving."

Then she continued with one of the few personal references that ever came into our conversations:

"I was not educated in a conventional way," she said, "owing to physical interruptions in my youth, but I believe that I have rather an unusual gift for absorption. My brother, Albert, was educated at Dartmouth College, and when he realized how eager I was for knowledge he made a point of sharing what he learned — particularly during the vacations at home. He used to say that I absorbed from him in a single vacation period as much as he had learned the previous term from textbooks. I have been absorbing ever since. That is what I mean when I say, 'You are giving and I am receiving.' "

This incident I feel is significant, for I place her power to absorb among her greatest personal assets, but the best part of it all was that while absorbing she was instinctively giving out again. Looking back at these conferences I can recall so many constructive comments and wise agreements or disagreements that were to make their truth evident at some future time, which, at the moment, seemed only a casual part of the general conversation.

The next manufacturing project for Mrs. Eddy came this same year, 1897. Mr. Armstrong advised me that Mrs. Eddy wished to see me as soon as it was convenient. As she was coming to Boston less frequently, she required a fuller personal account from time to time regarding the progress of her printing, so I anticipated merely a routine conference; but after these details were disposed of, she pointed to a package lying on the table. As I opened it, she remarked:

"I have a new manuscript for you. These are writings of mine that have appeared during the past years which I consider essential to preparing Christian Scientists for the full understanding of Science and Health. There is nothing to discuss about style, as I want the new book to match Science and Health in every way, but I do urge you to put it through the press as rapidly as possible because I am asking my students to cease teaching Christian Science until after the volume has appeared."

This was "Miscellaneous Writings." What she said, of course, gave me an idea of the importance she attached to the new volume, but I could not have known at the time that her injunction to her students prohibited the teaching of Christian Science for a year. Mrs. Eddy's reason for doing this is clearly shown in a notice published in *The Christian Science Journal* for March, 1897:

The Christian Scientists in the United States and Canada are hereby enjoined not to teach a student Christian Science for one year, commencing on March 14th, 1897.

"Miscellaneous Writings" is calculated to prepare the minds of all true thinkers to understand the Christian

Science Text-book more correctly than a student can.

The Bible, Science and Health with Key to the Scriptures, and my other published works, are the only proper instructors for this hour.

Exact, as always, Mrs. Eddy lifted the ban in the following notice, published in *The Christian Science Journal* for March, 1898:

I hereby notify the field that on March 1st the year expires in which Christian Scientists were requested to abstain from teaching. To-day my message to you is that loyal students from the Massachusetts Metaphysical College who have proven themselves good and useful teachers may instruct two classes of not over thirty (30) students during this ensuing year. May our God that is Love teach us this year and every year how to serve Him. May the dear, faithful laborers who are not required to teach this year, "Wait patiently on the Lord, and He will renew their strength" for that which is to come.

MARY BAKER G. EDDY.

When I had an opportunity to go over the manuscript at the Press, preparatory to putting it in the hands of the compositors, a realization came to me of how much more this extraordinary woman had accomplished — even beyond what I had witnessed with such accumulating admiration and amazement. I was familiar with her successful efforts to establish, singlehanded, a growing publishing business, which during its first fifteen years had produced and sold 61,000 copies of Science and Health, besides many thousands each of her other published shorter writings. I had witnessed personally the skill and diplomacy with which she held her course during the confusing years of her early experiment with the first two publishers, which saw Science and Health pass into its one hundred and tenth edition, and the writing and the publication of the Church Manual (1895), which was to become the mariners' chart for the policies primarily of The Mother Church, but indirectly of Christian Science churches throughout the world. Now, in addition to all that I had known, here in the manuscript of the new volume, "Miscellaneous Writings," was contained 150,000 words of expository messages to her students and followers, written during the crowded years of 1883–1896, which she considered so vital that she had requested her students for the time being to cease their teaching.

I have been interested, more recently, to check with the records to discover how much was still omitted in my knowledge of Mrs. Eddy's other activities prior to and during the period I had known her. This is what I find she had accomplished:

Created a governing Board to be known as The Christian Science Board of Directors, through a Deed of Trust dated September 1, 1892.

Organized The Mother Church, The First Church of Christ, Scientist, Boston, Massachusetts, in September, 1892.

Built the original edifice of The Mother Church 1893–1894.

Delivered an address in The Mother Church, May 26, 1895.

Delivered an address in The Mother Church, January 5, 1896.

Wrote her Message to The Mother Church in 1898.

Established The Christian Science Publishing Society, through a Deed of Trust dated January 25, 1898.

Taught her last Normal class in Concord, New Hampshire, in November, 1898.

Established a Christian Science Board of Lectureship in 1898.

Established a Christian Science Board of Education in 1898.

Spoke at the Annual Meeting in Tremont Temple on June 6, 1899.

Received annually at Pleasant View for several years large numbers of her followers.

Established the *Christian Science Sentinel.*

Carried on an extensive correspondence with the church officials of The Mother Church and with branch churches throughout the world.

Established the Bible and "Science and Health with Key to the Scriptures" as the only Pastor over The Mother Church and its branches.

Established the *Christian Science Quarterly* as it stands today.

Edited many of the editorials and articles in *The Christian Science Journal* and *Sentinel* written by others than herself.

During this same period, Mrs. Eddy had held herself

closely to the revision of each of the new editions
issued of Science and Health, which required the closest
application and study, as she strove to make her message
clearer. One would have expected that this alone would
have required her retirement to an Ivory Tower, but
her extraordinary gift of turning from temporal to
spiritual concentration somehow enabled her to carry
on the two conflicting responsibilities without permitting either to infringe upon the other. Mrs. Eddy
did not show the strain physically, she did not admit
it, but she was not unaware of it. In the Preface of
"Miscellaneous Writings," she says of this period:

To preserve a long course of years still and uniform,
amid the uniform darkness of storm and cloud and tempest,
requires strength from above, — deep draughts from the
fount of divine Love. Truly may it be said: There is an
old age of the heart, and a youth that never grows old; a
Love that is a boy, and a Psyche who is ever a girl. The
fleeting freshness of youth, however, is not the evergreen
of Soul; the coloring glory of perpetual bloom; the spiritual
glow and grandeur of a consecrated life wherein dwelleth
peace, sacred and sincere in trial or in triumph.

When I consider the sum total of her known labors
during that period, I cannot avoid asking myself what
other man or woman in all history ever equaled this
record. To me this is an unanswerable challenge, yet
all this was but a prelude to even more astonishing
accomplishments still to come!

With the office of publisher manned by a competent staff, which handled the increasing orders with business-like efficiency, Mrs. Eddy called me into conference occasionally but not so frequently during the two or three years which followed the publication of "Miscellaneous Writings." Throughout these conferences I always found her calm and deliberate, seemingly with no unusual burdens or responsibilities, and always urging me to tell her of the progress of my own work at the University Press, and to share with her the results of my increasingly intensive study of the artist master printers of the past. I really believed that at last she had reached a point where she felt that her objective was assured, and was settling back to view the developing picture with well-earned gratification.

In November, 1900, I wrote a letter to Mr. Armstrong which, looking backward, is of significance to this story in that it contains the first suggestion of a "sumptuous" edition of Science and Health — an idea which was to require forty years to turn into a reality. From this letter I take the following extracts:

The question of an edition of Science and Health following the style of the sample pages which were left with you yesterday, was suggested to the writer by the fact that during the last year or so he has heard the desire expressed by different Scientists among his friends for a larger and more attractive edition of Science and Health, suitable for gifts or for use in the home, similar to the old family Bible. In addition to this it seemed to him that such an edition as outlined would be of much value in the various churches, and, finally, that all Scientists would appreciate having the book given so fitting a setting. With this in mind we have set up the four pages which were left with you yesterday. Our idea would be to have 8 separate borders drawn which should be masterpieces of their kind, introducing decorations significant to Christian Science, these borders to be changed every four pages throughout the book, but repeating themselves after each 32. We would suggest that the borders be made slightly smaller than the sample border (which is merely decorative), allowing room on the inside of each border for type matter to run in large type, line for line with the regular edition, as this will be a useful arrangement as far as church work is concerned.

We should plan to use the very best quality of handmade paper throughout, watermarked "Science and Health," and printed in two colors all the way through. For binding we recommend full genuine vellum with brass clasps specially designed running over the side of the book and over the vellum in a decorative manner somewhat similar in effect to the old-fashioned hinges. Between these brass hinges we suggest handsome gold ornamentation of significant design.

In other words, what we plan is something after the style of the two volumes issued several years ago by the bishops of the Episcopal Church called the "Book of Common Prayer," and the "Holy Communion." The plan which we have suggested, however, contemplates a much handsomer book in every respect than these; and, in fact, it would be our endeavor to make this represent the highest expression of the printer's and binder's art.

Such in outline is the plan which we have to suggest. The writer has devoted much time and thought to the subject, and would very much appreciate an opportunity to go over the matter fully with you and Mrs. Eddy. If Mrs. Eddy should care to consider the matter at all, it would be much easier to show her exactly what we have in mind during a conversation than by correspondence, and he would also be glad to bring with him a copy of the Episcopal book which, together with our sample pages, would give, we think, a very clear idea of what could be accomplished.

Now that the new edition of Science and Health is contemplated would it not be a fitting time to consider the subject suggested above? If so, it would give the writer much pleasure to talk with you personally about it, if he might be permitted to do so, or to take it up in any such way as you might indicate.

Looking backwards, all this was premature and undeveloped, but it emphasizes to me how permanently the comment Mrs. Eddy had made to me eight years earlier, regarding beauty and the man, had taken root and was demanding expression. It also recalls how earnestly I wanted to demonstrate to Mrs. Eddy what her farseeing advice had meant to me in my professional life. Mr. Armstrong was courteous and sympathetic to the idea in general, but quite properly pointed out an insurmountable obstacle in that the text of Science and Health was still subject to changes by the author. In further explanation of my seeming lack of understanding, I might record that I thought I saw ahead of me in the near future an opportunity to visit Europe, and to continue my study of the work of the old master printers at its source. If the idea of a "sumptuous" edition of Science and Health appealed at all to Mrs. Eddy, I might make this the objective of my research and study. Mr. Armstrong did me the courtesy of showing my letter and sample material to Mrs. Eddy, but it was some time later that I learned from her that he had done so. Hearing nothing, of course I dropped the matter from my present consideration.

By this time I had affairs at the University Press well under control, and found that the time had come when I might make my long-anticipated trip to Europe. This was in 1901. I asked my various clients to advise me if they had any special problems of manufacture likely to come up during the three months' absence which might be discussed, in outline at least, before my departure. As a result of my letter to Mrs. Eddy, there came an immediate request for a conference at Concord at my convenience. It was a privilege to visit peaceful Pleasant View again after the longest interval that had occurred, and, as I made the journey from Boston, many happy memories came back to me of other meetings during the period since my earliest trip there as a youngster almost ten years before.

As I was shown into the study, I remember being impressed with the fact that so few changes seemed to have been made during the entire period: the furniture must have been altered and rearranged, there must have been changes in the house and grounds, but if so all had been so gradual that everything seemed the same to me. And the most extraordinary fact, which struck me more forcibly than during our meetings in Boston, was the lack of change in Mrs. Eddy herself. When she entered the room, just as she had done on that first visit of mine, she seemed just as she had always seemed: the same bright smile of welcome, the same penetrating, assessing eyes, the same alertness of manner, the same clear, musical voice, the same physical vigor I had always remembered — yet the ten years that had been added to the history of the world had added the same number of years to this slight little woman — years of conflict and triumph, years of disappointment and gratification, years of consecration and of arduous labor, years of achievement and accomplishment — and had left no visible mark. Mrs. Eddy was eighty years old at the time, and had summoned me to discuss with her not some trivial detail associated with her business, but to make definite arrangements for the consummation of her long-determined plan to place the finishing touch on her textbook as her bequest to the world, and further plans to make the volume more available. During that concentrated, detailed discussion there was never the slightest evidence of uncertainty or of fatigue.

Before the conference began, she surprised me by
saying, "I was sorry to disappoint you in the matter
of that beautiful edition of Science and Health you
wanted to make. I am pleased that you wish to do this
for me; but Mr. Armstrong was right, the time has
not come."

Then she turned at once to my personal plans for
Europe. "So you are really going to gratify your
desire," she said, smiling. "You have been very patient,
but I hope you feel that the delay has been worth while."

"Yes," I admitted, still a bit begrudgingly; "and if
my work abroad results in giving me a chance to add
something to the quality of American bookmaking, I
shall be sure of it — but I still want to write!"

I think Mrs. Eddy was surprised to find how firmly
the old obsession still held me, for her voice became
more serious as she replied:

"If you feel that urge so strongly, you *will* write.
Nothing can stop you, and the longer and deeper you
have lived, the more worth while your writing will
be. You are a young man still, and can afford to be
patient."

I could not wholly accept Mrs. Eddy's optimistic
statement at the time, but when I glance at the list
of thirty-odd titles of published volumes which bear
my name as author — books written "in between" the
demands of a full business life and the social responsibilities of personal living — I can but record, as I have

already done again and again, how very right Mrs. Eddy always seemed to be!

As the conversation turned back to my proposed European trip, Mrs. Eddy inquired when I expected to return. On receiving the information she was thoughtful for a moment, then she said:

"That will fit in perfectly with my plans. When you return I shall need your assistance. I have been working on what will be my final revision of Science and Health, except perhaps for later verbal changes, and this means resetting the entire book. There will be new problems in the typography, for I want the lines to be numbered. My dear friends and students, Mr. Kimball and Mr. McKenzie, are working with me, and when the new plates are finally completed, Mr. Conant will prepare a comprehensive Concordance that will replace the Index, and make the textbook more easily available to its readers."

The simplicity of this announcement did not blind me to the vastness of her project. A short half-hour before I had thought that this calm little woman sitting in front of me was settling back to watch the fulfillment of her plans, when as a matter of fact she was at that moment involved in elaborate preparations for the coming year which would demand of her actual spiritual and physical labor — in concentration and writing, to say nothing of her meticulous supervision — even beyond what she had given in years gone by!

I left Pleasant View with wonder and admiration in my heart, and with her best wishes for a happy voyage and a productive European trip. A month later I was on board the tiny 5,000-ton "Lahn" of the North German Lloyd Line, bound for Naples.

A reference to this trip to Europe, the first of twenty pilgrimages to the Old World for study and inspiration, has its place in this story for three reasons: first, because it introduced me to Dr. Guido Biagi, at that time Librarian of the Riccardi and the Laurentian Libraries in Florence, and Custodian of the Medici, the Michelangelo, and the da Vinci Archives, who was to become one of the three personalities who profoundly affected my professional life, the other two being Mrs. Eddy, and Charles Eliot Norton of Harvard University; second, because except for Dr. Biagi there would have been no Laurentian type; and third, because except for the Laurentian type, and what I learned about designing and printing while producing the Laurentian type, there would have been no Subscription Edition of Science and Health. The influence of each of these three friends came from a different angle, yet in the joint effect the three were closely interwoven.

Before I give you Dr. Biagi, I must draw a picture of his frame, because Dr. Biagi and the Laurentian in my mind are one and inseparable. My first "must" when I reached Florence was a visit to this famous library. I made use of the entrance at the extreme right, and found myself within the old Church of San Lorenzo. Passing between the heavy crimson curtains I was instantly transported from the twentieth to the fifteenth century. As I looked around, in the dim light, I recognized the bronze pulpit from which Savonarola had warned his fellow Florentines against the intrigues of the Medici, knowing full well the penalty of such insolence toward the powerful ruling family.

Walking down the nave I veered off to the left and entered the Old Sacristy, then from there into the so-called "New" Sacristy — new yet built over four centuries ago. Here was Michelangelo's tomb for Lorenzo the Magnificent, guarded by those great masterpieces "Day and Night" and "Dawn and Twilight."

From the Martelli Chapel I went out into the cloister, feeling the need of a breath of air after the heavy atmosphere of the church. From the cloister I mounted an ancient stone staircase, and found myself at the foot of one of the most famous stairways in the world. At the top I paused for a moment before entering the great hall, the *Sala di Michelangiolo*. Here I was greeted by the attendant, to whom I presented my letter of introduction to the Librarian. Bowing low, he asked me to follow him. In passing down the length of the hall I saw the Librarian for the first time, seated at one of the *plutei*, studying a Medicean illuminated manuscript fastened to the desk by one of the famous old chains.

Dr. Biagi was a Tuscan, rather heavily built, and of medium height. His forehead was high, and his eyes kindly and alert. His full beard made him appear older than he was. I was captivated at once by the combination of his musical Italian voice, his assessing eyes, and his appealing smile. A letter of introduction such as mine, was, of course, an everyday affair to him, and I have no doubt that he expected, as I did, that our meeting that day might result in my receiving a few additional courtesies; but neither of us realized, I am sure, that the meeting was to be so vitally significant — that this man was to become my closest friend, and that through him the Laurentian Library was to become for me a sanctuary. During the twenty-five years that elapsed between that day and his passing, we were not only friends but fellow students, and I can never be sufficiently grateful for the generosity with which he permitted me to draw upon the vast store of knowledge he possessed.

From Biagi I learned for the first time of the tremendous importance of the Humanistic movement, starting with Petrarch in the thirteenth century, culminating in the rescue of the classic manuscripts from destruction, and holding them in readiness to be duplicated by the coming invention of printing, which was still to be born.

Aside from his position as the leading librarian in Italy, Biagi ranked high among the Italian intellectuals

as the author of important books, as the outstanding
Dante scholar, and as a lecturer on various erudite subjects, first among which was that of humanism, to
which he had just introduced me. He found in me
a ready listener.

"A humanist," he explained, "is neither master of
fate, nor victim of fate, but is co-partner with Nature
in solving his personal problem."

Later, in answer to my query, he gave me a
more detailed definition. "The humanist," he enlarged,
"whether ancient or modern, is one who holds himself
open to receive Truth unprejudiced as to its source,
and — what is more important — having received Truth,
realizes his obligation to the world to give it out again,
made richer by his personal interpretation."

It was this discussion which led me to talk with
him of Mrs. Eddy, for there seemed to me to be much
in the philosophy of humanism which tied in with
what I had unconsciously absorbed of Mrs. Eddy's
philosophy of Christian Science. Biagi listened attentively. He was particularly interested when I repeated
to him what Mrs. Eddy had said to me when she
explained why she wished to have a Bible-paper edition
of Science and Health! "It has always been my desire
that my book should encourage more and more people
to read the Bible."

"If her book can do that," Biagi exclaimed emphati-
cally, "it is a masterpiece. The Bible is the one source

of health and life, and people don't know how to use it. I am greatly interested in what you tell me. We in Italy would surely consider Mrs. Eddy a humanist. Will you send me a copy of her book, Science and Health? I should like to study it."

Thus it was that during subsequent visits Dr. Biagi never failed to inquire about Mrs. Eddy, and I know he read Science and Health carefully and with profound interest and sympathy.

The first seed of the Laurentian type was sown during this visit, but it required four years and two further trips to Italy to bring the seed to flower. In the section of this book devoted to the dramatic story of the Subscription Edition of Science and Health fuller details will be given, but the record of the birth of the type belongs here.

When it became evident that Gutenberg's invention of printing made it possible to produce books mechanically, the princely houses realized at once that if the masses could learn to read, the political power which lay vested in them was definitely threatened. For that reason they did everything in their power to prevent the growth of the art of printing. With this in mind, during the last quarter of the fifteenth century, such rulers as the House of Medici gave more elaborate orders for hand-lettered volumes to the private scribes than in all the history of calligraphy. So it happened that during this limited period hand-lettering reached a degree of perfection never before attained, and the manuscripts thus produced became known as "humanistic." The Laurentian, over which Dr. Biagi presided, contains more copies of these manuscripts than any other single library. Biagi proudly showed me some of these treasures, notably Antonio Sinibaldi's "Virgil." The contrast between the hand-lettering in these volumes and the best I had ever seen before was startling. The humanistic letter, developed under unusually dramatic and romantic conditions, really represented the apotheosis of the hand-letterer's art. Up to this point all types in existence had been based upon the models of hand-lettering less beautiful and not nearly so perfect in execution.

"Why is it," I demanded of Biagi excitedly, "that no type has ever been designed based upon hand-lettering at its highest point of perfection?"

Biagi looked at me a moment, and then characteristically shrugged his shoulders. "This, my friend," he answered, "is your opportunity."

I suppose at some time in his life every book designer experiences the ambition to design a special type, and Dr. Biagi's suggestion appealed to me with great force. It was all experimental, but it gave me an interesting excuse to extend my stay in Florence. I confined myself at first to a study of the humanistic volumes in the Laurentian Library, and the selection of the best examples to be taken as final models for the various letters. Then I had pages of these manuscripts photographed and enlarged for later study. This was as far as I could go for the time being, but, having possessed myself of these photographs, I left Dr. Biagi almost as excited as I was, and with every encouragement to come back and receive his assistance when I had delved more deeply into the possibilities of carrying the experiment to a conclusion.

On my return to America, I at once put myself in touch with Mrs. Eddy, and found that the work on the proposed revision of Science and Health was practically completed, and the manuscript was about ready to be turned over to me. Naturally I was overflowing with eagerness to discuss my new adventure with Mrs. Eddy, but I promptly placed that idea aside when I saw how completely she was absorbed in giving of herself to this polishing and rounding out of the final revision of the textbook. I was delighted to find that at long last adequate protection was being given to Mrs. Eddy, so that no extraneous subject should interfere with her concentration, or add an ounce of additional weight to her self-assumed burden. All this, too, was further evidence that Mrs. Eddy's affairs as a whole were being administered more to her liking. Her key men had proved themselves loyal and efficient, and while she never for a moment relinquished the

all-seeing eye of supervision, her power of accomplishment was increased definitely by this co-operation.

I was interested also to find that she had delegated
William P. McKenzie rather than Mr. Armstrong to
discuss with me such details as sample type pages, as
this new edition would have seemed to be the responsibility of the publisher. I did not know until later
how much Mrs. Eddy was placing upon Mr. Armstrong,
outside his normal functions as publisher, in connection
with the maturing and sometimes troublesome details
associated with Church affairs.

This was my first meeting with Mr. McKenzie, and
proved to be the beginning of a lifelong friendship,
which I consider an additional dividend to the many
that have accrued to me from my association with the
printing of Mrs. Eddy's books. He was a rare man,
deeply interested in the humanities, with a spiritual
character which I have never ceased to admire.

As he and I went over the manuscript together, it
became evident what hours of concentrated thought
had gone into its revision. Mr. McKenzie pointed out
to me that not less than half the pages contained corrections — a word here, a rearranged sentence there, a dele-
tion, or an elaboration — never a change of thought,
but finally expressing the author's mature judgment in
making the meaning clearer and more easily absorbed.
The chapters had been rearranged, the side headings
revised, and a new chapter, "Fruitage," was added. The

material for this chapter had been selected by Mr. McKenzie and Edward A. Kimball from a large collection of testimonies turned over to them by Mrs. Eddy with instructions to select the most significant. They also checked the quotations, and brought to Mrs. Eddy's attention during the revision points which they thought might be further clarified. I was not surprised, in view of what Mrs. Eddy had confided to me of her plans for Mr. Conant's comprehensive Concordance, that the index originally made by Mr. Wiggin was dropped. With the deletions and additions we now had a volume of some seven hundred pages, and it was to appear as the two hundred and twenty-sixth thousand, the word *thousand* now being used for the previous word *edition*.

The first problem on the manuscript was to determine just how to handle the numbering of the lines in preparation for the coming Concordance. Mr. McKenzie's idea was to place the figure after each line, but I explained to him that the solid column of figures lined up against the text on each page would not only be a blemish typographically, but would divert the reader from the text itself. At first I thought it would accomplish the purpose to place figures opposite each fifth line, but that proved too open, and we settled finally on tagging each third line. Mr. McKenzie suggested taking the three experimental pages to Mrs. Eddy. I told him that she always preferred a definite suggestion rather than alternative choices.

"Put the proofs in your pocket," I said, "but show her the one you and I prefer, holding the other proofs in reserve. I don't think she will ask for them."

Later we laughed together over his experience with Mrs. Eddy. "You were entirely right," he chuckled. "She looked at the proof carefully, then she said, 'That is exactly right,' and we passed on to other details."

With this important innovation satisfactorily established, Mr. McKenzie and I took up the general layout of the typography in the book itself. Fashions in bookmaking change from time to time just as they do in clothing, and this was a period when the introduction of typesetting machines had resulted in producing an unusually wide choice in type faces. Mrs. Eddy was always interested in new developments of any kind, and when I talked with her just before my European trip, we discussed this very point. Mr. Wilson had established a basis for sound, old-fashioned typography which had been strictly adhered to in the resettings that followed. The question was, should we remain old-fashioned in planning the new edition, or should we bring the new volume typographically up to date?

"A book is like a friend," Mrs. Eddy said definitely. "We become familiar with a friend's face, and keep the well-known features fixed in our mind. I think readers of Science and Health would be a little shocked to see the pages with which they are so familiar appear now in a different form."

She was right, and this is the reason that the type pages of the textbook have been kept so uniform in succeeding editions, the reflection of the more modern presentation being confined to the front matter, the arrangement of type at the beginning of chapters, and to the running heads.

Mr. McKenzie was a delightful man to work with, and this helped to mitigate in part the realization that the days of my closer contacts with Mrs. Eddy were now inevitably bound to be limited. This of course was as it must be, but youth is always eager for more of those happy experiences which have already been given him in too generous measure. Frankly, I found myself half envious of Mr. McKenzie as he shuttled back and forth between us! But there were compensations. As our friendship developed, Mr. McKenzie enlarged on the messages of greeting and appreciation that Mrs. Eddy so kindly sent me by him in between pages of proof, and he repeated to me references she had made to our earlier association which could never have come to me otherwise, and which I shall always cherish. His curiosity was obviously aroused by these messages.

"Mrs. Eddy seems to be unusually interested in your career," he remarked one day, with a rising inflection in his voice.

I confided in part my relations with her during the preceding years. Mr. McKenzie gave me a friendly smile. "That would explain it," he said. "She evidently feels that she has influenced your work, and is pleased with the way you have accepted her suggestions."

This made the waiting for the opportunity to talk over the new type design in person with Mrs. Eddy easier for my youthful enthusiasm, which was so eager to express itself!

This 1902 edition of Science and Health met with the approval of Mrs. Eddy and her collaborators from every angle, and naturally the demand for copies of the new volume was exceedingly heavy. During the following three years the notation on the back of the title page was continued, but in 1906 Mrs. Eddy decided to drop the numbering of the editions, as the book was now so universally accepted as the standard and only textbook on Christian Science that the extent of its distribution became unimportant as a matter of record. The last numbered editions, four hundred and seventeenth in cloth, and four hundred and eighteenth in limp leather, appeared in 1906, bearing the Armstrong imprint as publisher.

Immediately after the 1902 revised edition of Science and Health passed out of her hands, the indefatigable author turned to the consideration of the copy for the Concordance. This resulted in a call for a personal conference with Mrs. Eddy at Concord, to decide how this copy should be prepared to make it intelligent to the typesetter in the combination of bold face and roman type to differentiate between the various entries, and thus keep the references easy of access for the reader. The summons for the conference came through Mr. Armstrong with a notation which made me very happy: "Mrs. Eddy requests that you bring with you the drawings of your new type." Mr. McKenzie had evidently told her about my adventure!

Again the familiar scene and the happily remembered Pleasant View! Our meeting was unusually cordial after the long break. Mrs. Eddy showed none of the strain she must have labored under throughout the period since I had last seen her. After the first greeting, she said:

"I hope Mr. McKenzie has made it clear to you how pleased I am with the new edition. This was made under the conditions of a definite plan supervised by a single mind, just as you discussed with me long ago, and the results demonstrate the rightness of your plan. Today we have to talk about the Concordance. In making that book, you will be dealing with Mr. Conant, who will join us in half an hour — but first I want to hear about your new type."

It was amazing that she had even remembered Mr. McKenzie's suggestion that there was a new type in the offing! But this was definitely characteristic. Mrs. Eddy had so consecrated her life to a single purpose that many misinterpreted the barrier she was obliged to establish between herself and the outside world as aloofness, when in reality it was absolutely required for self-defense. There could be no place in her life, as she had ordained to organize it, for friendships in the conventional sense. Knowing her nature as I did, I feel that this sacrifice must have required unusual courage to recognize and accept. Yet when, as in the present instance, there was something that definitely interested her, she had the unusual gift of interpolating it without allowing it to divert her from her plotted path. This was an expression of the great humanity this unusual woman possessed but kept ever under control, and it was this human touch that tempered her spiritual interpretations, making them, it seems to me, that much the more easily understood by those she sought to serve.

And so this half-hour, so generously given and so gratefully accepted, was devoted to subjects far afield from the Concordance to Science and Health! I told Mrs. Eddy of the Laurentian Library and the influence it exerted on all who worked there, and became subject to its historic and literary atmosphere: I introduced Guido Biagi to her, and related what he had said concerning the subject of humanism, and his reaction that it was akin to her own philosophy. I hoped she would make some comment in response, but she only said:

"That is most interesting. If you hear from him after he has read Science and Health, I should be glad to know what he said."

When I handed her 'the enlarged drawings for the Humanistic type, she examined them critically for several moments.

"They are beautiful," she said at length — "beautiful and not ornate, and they are distinctly legible. In using this type I am sure you will not make the mistake William Morris did of overloading it with decoration."

Then I shared with her the early comments on the design made by Charles Eliot Norton, in a letter:

There can be little question that your experiment is in the right direction. Most modern type lacks freshness and individuality, but examination of the new font shows its contrast to the familiar, dry, mechanical type. There is attractive freedom and unusual grace in its lines, derived immediately from the manuscript volumes, but adapted to the necessarily rigid requirements of the printer.

I explained to Mrs. Eddy that Professor Norton referred to the fact that I had not undertaken to produce an Orcutt type. It would have been presumptuous for anyone to attempt to improve on hand-lettering which was recognized as the finest ever produced. I sought rather to preserve the artistic design and the marvelous skill of the humanistic scribes by translating a beautiful thing from one medium into another. Any credit which might come to me would not be from the design itself, but from whatever degree of success I might achieve in reproducing the original with some degree of fidelity.

Mrs. Eddy listened attentively to all this explanation, and a broad smile came to her face as she remarked quietly, "I approved your approach to the designing of this type even before you explained it to me, and what I wrote was long before Professor Norton put it into his own words." Then she quoted from Science and Health (p. 310):

The artist is not in his painting. The picture is the artist's thought objectified. The human belief fancies that it delineates thought on matter, but what is matter? Did it exist prior to thought? Matter is made up of supposititious mortal mind-force; but all might is divine Mind. Thought will finally be understood and seen in all form, substance, and color, but without material accompaniments. The potter is not in the clay; else the clay would have power over the potter. God is His own infinite Mind, and expresses all.

It was a wonderful privilege to listen to Mrs. Eddy's clear, musical voice as she recited these lines from the textbook. The only time I ever experienced a similar sensation was a few years earlier when, as one of the few privileged guests at Julia Ward Howe's eightieth birthday party, at her home on Beacon Street, Boston, I heard another great woman recite from her own writings, this time the "Battle Hymn of the Republic."

My allotted period was at an end. Mr. Conant was summoned to join us, and the conversation then shifted to the subject of the Concordance as naturally as if

Mrs. Eddy and I had been discussing nothing else. Her ability to change from one topic to another with such consummate ease continued to amaze me. The earlier subject was not left hanging in the air but was completely finished, at least for the time being. When that topic came to be taken up again, Mrs. Eddy would make the contact with perfect accuracy, and would carry on from the previous point as if the discussion had never been interrupted. Abraham Lincoln is said to have possessed this ability to a similar degree.

Albert F. Conant, to whom Mrs. Eddy had assigned the task of compiling the Concordance to Science and Health, was an entirely different type from Mr. McKenzie, with whom I had worked out the problems of the newly reset edition of the textbook. Mr. Conant's interests were along statistical rather than literary lines, which qualified him eminently for his present undertaking; and he did a magnificent piece of work. Mrs. Eddy had shown rare judgment in her selection of these two men from whom she was asking such different services. As soon as the plates of the 1902 edition of Science and Health were cast, thus "freezing" the numbered lines, Mr. Conant had started work on his copy for the compositors to follow in translating it into type. He had prepared experimental cards covering the nouns, verbs, adjectives, and adverbs in Science and Health, each noun being provided with sub-references. These cards Mrs. Eddy wished us to discuss in her presence, to determine the use of bold face or roman type in sizes which established at a glance the classification to which each word belonged. She and Mr. Conant had, of course, discussed these points at length prior to our meeting. Mr. Conant did all the explaining with but an occasional comment from Mrs. Eddy. I made careful notes on which to base my sample pages, which were to be prepared and submitted, and the conference was at an end. Mrs. Eddy had satisfied herself that Mr. Conant had presented the matter to me *exactly* as she wished it!

Ironically, the University Press was not to do the typesetting on this book after all! There were certain bold-face types Mrs. Eddy wished to have used which the University Press did not have in stock. These were located at the Riverside Press, in Cambridge, to which we entrusted the work. At Mrs. Eddy's request, I passed on the sample pages, checked the proof, and, when the plates were complete, received them at the University Press for printing.

In 1906 I made my third Odyssey to Europe. My itinerary included a visit to Parma, Italy, to study the work of Giambattista Bodoni, the most glamorous figure in the typographical Hall of Fame. It was not until I visited the Palatine Library in Parma, and found there, thanks to the gracious courtesy of Dr. Pietro Zorzanello, the scholarly Librarian, an opportunity to study at my leisure the complete set of Bodoni volumes, together with the actual punches and matrices which Bodoni left, that I fully realized what a great influence Bodoni had exercised in placing his profession squarely among the Fine Arts.

The height of Bodoni's fame came at the very turn of the nineteenth century. King Carlos III appointed him Royal Printer to Spain. Pensions were granted to him by Napoleon Bonaparte and other potentates. Special medals were struck by the cities of Paris and Parma in his honor. He could not move about without attracting attention, and no person of consequence passed through Parma without including the Bodoni printing establishment as one of the places of greatest interest.

But it is the Bodoni type which plays its part in this narrative. I was much struck by its beauty and dignity. As Bodoni himself described it, "The type shall represent the beautiful contrast as between light and shade which comes naturally from any writing done with a well-cut pen held properly in the hand." It is not fair to judge the Bodoni design from the fonts which have been recut in America. Bodoni had no idea of creating a popular type, and when the type founders and the typesetting machines tried to make it so, they robbed it of the very characteristics which gave it beauty. Bodoni laid out his books with extravagantly wide margins, with liberal spacing between the lines of type. He did not hesitate, therefore, to lengthen the ascending and descending strokes of his letters, as he never intended to set his type solid.

As I studied this type, it seemed to me to be exactly the one which would make my still-cherished "sumptuous" edition of Science and Health a masterpiece! It had been used to produce beautiful editions of various classics, and it had been acclaimed by princes and potentates. Surely, here was a type worthy to be selected for the pretentious purpose I had in mind. The punches and the matrices belonged to the Italian Government, but, with the assistance of the American Ambassador, George von L. Meyer, governmental permission to have the type cast and shipped to America was granted.

As a result of all this, I returned home with the urge for the "sumptuous" edition of Science and Health rekindled. I had pages of Science and Health set up, and rejoiced to find that the new type enabled me to set the page line for line. I had a special border designed, and, with apologies for my persistence, again took the matter up with Mr. Armstrong.

This time I found him more interested than in 1900, as the type appealed to him strongly, and the decorations set off the type in a handsome manner. Moreover, this was seven years later than my original proposal, and Science and Health was just that much nearer to being freed from the necessity of further alterations. I was delighted, therefore, when he volunteered to take these samples to Mrs. Eddy, and I really felt encouraged when he reported to me that she was interested to the extent of designating Archibald McLellan to go into the details more fully with me. This was in the early fall of 1907. I again attacked the problem with renewed enthusiasm, but before the project could be further advanced, Mr. Armstrong passed away, and of course all negotiations were dropped for the time being.

Allison V. Stewart became Mr. Armstrong's successor as publisher in 1907, and this matter of the "sumptuous" edition was the first important consideration to which he fell heir. Mr. Stewart came from Chicago, where he had been engaged in the public practice of Christian Science, and was also serving as Christian Science Committee on Publication for the State of Illinois. On the occasion of one of my earliest meetings with him, he told me Mrs. Eddy had asked him to take Mr. Armstrong's place in conferences with Mr. McLellan, so it really looked as if the project was moving favorably. On March 11, 1908, therefore, I placed the whole matter before her in the following letter:

DEAR MRS. EDDY: — Agreeably to your suggestions after receiving my letter last November, I took up with Mr. McLellan and Mr. Armstrong details regarding the sumptuous edition of Science and Health which I suggested, showing them the tentative sample pages, decorations, suggestions for binding, etc., with which they were much pleased. Later I submitted to Mr. McLellan and Mr. Stewart the final sample page containing one of the identical borders which I suggest using, again going over the details with the actual samples before us, — all of which I am glad to say met with their approval subject to your approbation. Everything therefore is now in shape to be shown to you, and I am sending you with this:

(a) The sample page
(b) Original design for a second border
(c) A copy of the Episcopal "Book of Common Prayer," showing general scheme for binding
(d) A sample of Kelmscott vellum which I suggest using for binding
(e) A copy of the Humanistic "Petrarch," to which reference will be made later.

After you have made an examination of these exhibits I sincerely trust that you will allow me to talk the matter over with you in person, as there is much which has vital bearing which cannot be indicated in a letter. As a basis, however, I beg to submit the following details: —

TYPE: The type shown in the sample page is a special face which has never been used except by the celebrated Italian printer, Bodoni, previous to the year 1800. The Italian Government owns all the matrices, but has granted us the sole privilege to its modern use. This makes it absolutely unique.

DECORATIONS: The border used on the printed sample page, together with the original design for a second border, will show you the general scheme. I suggest making eight different designs, all in harmony, to be reproduced in pairs, and repeating themselves after the first 16 pages. The present sample runs exactly page for page with the regular edition. Besides the borders there would be a designed title-page, and other decorations wherever appropriate.

PAPER: This would be specially made by hand of the best possible quality.

PRESSWORK: This would be in red and black throughout. We should plan to make this portion of the work, as all other portions, represent the highest degree of excellence which the art of printing has shown.

BINDING: I send you as a general suggestion a copy of "The Book of Common Prayer," issued by the bishops of the Episcopal Church. My plan is to use heavy boards, as here, covered with Kelmscott vellum — a sample of which is sent you. Upon the vellum I should stamp a heavy embellishment in gold, making the design symbolic and perhaps using the new design of the cross and crown in the centre. The book would have brass clasps.

CANCELS: It will be quite possible to print 4-page cancels for this edition, just as we do now for the regular one, so that any later changes may be included. Moreover, the composition can be so handled as to include, before printing, any changes made by you during the time of manufacture.

TIME: The volume would require six months in manufacture, as each process must be performed and supervised deliberately.

IN GENERAL: All this is but an outline. As I wrote you before, the book offers wonderful possibilities to the artist printer, and gives an opportunity to construct a typographical monument which shall stand as an example of the best when compared with what the Master Printers of the past have accomplished.

The "Petrarch" which I send for you to see is a book which we recently issued for Messrs. Little, Brown & Co. which sold for $40.00, and you will see by comparison how much more imposing the proposed edition of Science and Health is. More than this, the "Petrarch" sold purely on its typographical format, without any particular interest in the subject matter, which would be another argument distinctly in favor of the new edition of Science and Health. Of the "Petrarch" we have also manufactured a few copies upon vellum, with hand illumination, and if I may be permitted I shall take much pleasure in showing you our copy (which President [Theodore] Roosevelt called at our office to examine when he was in Boston a year ago) and explain to you further the possibilities which may exist along these lines. I have put so much thought into the matter that I have developed a degree of enthusiasm which I know you will pardon. The idea appeals to me considerably beyond its commercial aspects, and I very much anticipate the privilege of *telling* you what you must otherwise read between the lines. I shall be in Cambridge except from March 18th through March 23rd. May I not see you either before or soon after these dates?

Thanking you for the interest which you have already shown in this matter, and trusting that what I am sending you may seem to you to contain as many possibilities as I myself seem to see in them.

No direct answer to this letter came from Mrs. Eddy, but on April 2, 1908, I received a communication

from the Board of Directors, saying that it was not
deemed expedient to go on with the project at this
time. With the receipt of this, I decided that my
enthusiasm had carried me too far in my hope of ever
making a "sumptuous" edition of Science and Health,
and I placed the idea entirely out of my mind, not
foreseeing that thirty years later my fondest hopes were
to be realized.

Naturally at the time this was a bitter disappointment, but no more fortunate thing could have happened to me or to the plan than to have Mrs. Eddy
decide against it at that moment. The book, as I
visualized it then, would have been beautiful in itself,
but it would not have represented Science and Health,
nor Mrs. Eddy, nor myself, as it does today. The
years that were to intervene brought much to me in
my own development, so that when the right moment
came in 1939, I had that much the more to give.

The opening of the year 1907 seemed to show
Mrs. Eddy's affairs to be in a supremely satisfactory
state. At long last those nearest to her had succeeded
in securing for her an adequate isolation. She was
supplemented in her personal work by competent secretaries and typists; in her church affairs and business
enterprises she was surrounded by loyal and efficient
collaborators. New churches were being established
everywhere with thousands of new members.

As far as the printing of her books was concerned, Mr. Stewart was supplementing and anticipating every wish. The editions of the various titles succeeded each other with increasing regularity, but even as late as this nothing beyond routine was done without Mrs. Eddy's full knowledge and approval. She had reached the age of eighty-six, but no one who knew Mrs. Eddy could visualize inactivity as being associated with her at any age. The co-operation simply enabled her to accomplish that much more, and to continue the expansion and effectiveness of Christian Science beyond anything her followers could have conceived.

Everything seemed to be moving serenely when out of a clear sky the storm broke over the "Next Friends Suit" brought against Mrs. Eddy in March, 1907, which was to prove the unhappiest experience she had been forced to meet. This was a suit brought allegedly in Mrs. Eddy's interest by her son, George W. Glover, and other relatives, seeking to declare her incompetent to care for her property and questioning the loyalty of those around her. The petition sought to transfer the control and administration of Mrs. Eddy's extensive business affairs into the hands of the petitioners.

I doubt if anyone associated with Mrs. Eddy at that time was more distinctly shocked than those of us at the University Press. We had become familiar, through the years, with Mrs. Eddy's indefatigable energy and continuing activity in connection with the

revision of each new edition of Science and Health.
The shock was intensified by our definite knowledge
of the malicious nature of the attack. Within the period
when the citation charged Mrs. Eddy with being mentally incompetent to conduct her business affairs, we
had received through Mr. Stewart communications and
alterations written in her unforgettable hand which in
themselves should have been sufficient evidence to dis-
miss the suit. I followed the case with intense interest,
and rejoiced to see how, in this hour of need, her
strength was more than sufficient to turn her accusers
into objects of public ridicule.

I found Mr. Stewart a delightful man with whom
to work out the manufacturing problems as they arose,
and gradually a personal friendship developed which
I thoroughly enjoyed. We met outside of office hours,
and many a vexatious business question was solved in
between strokes of our golf clubs on the links of The
Country Club in Brookline, Massachusetts. Both Mr.
Stewart and his wife possessed the gracious gift of
humor, which added much to the pleasure of their
acquaintanceship. This leads me to record here an
amusing but significant incident.

There was a fellow member of The Country Club,
whom I will call Dr. Scott. I knew him very well,
and, because of the many sterling qualities he possessed,
I had come to overlook a brusqueness of manner which

amounted almost to rudeness and even ill manners. He possessed several well-developed aversions, but the greatest of these was Christian Science. Knowing that I was closely associated with the publishing of Mrs. Eddy's books, he took particular delight in taking me to task for what he termed being "an accessory after the fact." Sometimes our discussions waxed quite warm, as I did not hesitate to defend the consistency and sincerity of those who accepted Mrs. Eddy's teaching, to which I had been a witness from such close association.

It so happened that Mrs. Stewart suffered a fall in her Brookline home which resulted in a broken arm. Someone suggested sending for Dr. Scott, and he answered the call promptly. It was not until the bone was set and the bandages applied that some chance remark revealed the fact that the Stewarts were Christian Scientists. Dr. Scott at once began to bristle:

"So you are a Christian Scientist!" he exclaimed. "I wouldn't have come if I had known that. Why don't you treat yourself?"

The Stewarts, far from being annoyed by his rudeness, were amused. "Our Leader admonishes us to make use of surgical assistance in the case of broken bones," Mrs. Stewart replied with a smile.

"I don't believe a word of it," Dr. Scott retorted. "Show me where Mrs. Eddy ever gave any such counsel."

Mrs. Stewart picked up a copy of Science and Health from the table nearby and turning to page 401, read: "Until the advancing age admits the efficacy and supremacy of Mind, it is better for Christian Scientists to leave surgery and the adjustment of broken bones and dislocations to the fingers of a surgeon, while the mental healer confines himself chiefly to mental reconstruction and to the prevention of inflammation."

Dr. Scott reached for the book and slowly read the lines. As he laid the volume down, Mrs. Stewart could not resist extending to him the retort courteous: "There are a great many other paragraphs that I think would interest you, Dr. Scott. May I send you a copy with my compliments?"

Dr. Scott was distinctly sobered. He replied in a quiet tone of voice: "Not yet. But I thank you for showing me what you did. Perhaps I haven't fully understood."

"May I treat my arm, too?" Mrs. Stewart inquired.

"Yes, if you don't meddle with my bandages."

Later Dr. Scott sought me out at The Country Club and told me this story just as I have related it, but with an interesting addition: "I am not ready yet to talk to anyone but you, but this case has me on the ropes. I attached no importance to my patient's request to treat herself, but I have never seen a broken bone knit together so quickly or so perfectly. It has given me something to think about. Don't you tell anyone, but I have bought a copy of Science and Health, and I am going to find out what it is all about. There is something here we doctors don't understand."

When Mrs. Eddy moved from Concord, New Hampshire, to Chestnut Hill, Massachusetts, in January, 1908, I realized that this change was made to secure for her greater seclusion after the unhappy notoriety of the "Next Friends Suit," and I doubted if I should ever have another personal conference with her. From a business standpoint there was no real necessity. The increasing authority given by her to her Board of Directors of The Mother Church and Board of Trustees of The Christian Science Publishing Society, and the efficient manner in which Mr. Stewart carried out the Directors' instructions, resulted in a business routine which ran with ease and precision. Occasionally Mr. Stewart would bring me some happy little message from Mrs. Eddy, but it was obvious that at last a well-earned peace had settled over the remaining years of this extraordinary woman. Peace — but never inactivity! She must have been gratified by the rounding out of her ambitious but ever confident conception of her Church, but with Mrs. Eddy nothing ever remained static.

Even now, at eighty-seven years of age, she visualized an even wider horizon. Six months after settling in her new home, she confided to her Directors her plans for a daily newspaper. A month later, her Board of Trustees was instructed to proceed with plans to establish it, and still three months later, on November 25, 1908, *The Christian Science Monitor* was presented to the world, as she herself described it, "to injure no man, but to bless all mankind" (The First Church of Christ, Scientist, and Miscellany, p. 353).

Archibald McLellan was selected by Mrs. Eddy to become the first editor of *The Christian Science Monitor*, and he thus perhaps came into closer personal relation with her in founding the paper than anyone else. While lunching with him one day, not long after the paper was fairly launched, I was much interested to have him inquire as to the extent to which Mrs. Eddy entered into the details in the manufacture of her books. I answered his question freely, because, as I have already recorded, her power to plan out and follow through had always amazed me. I surmised that in the matter of the *Monitor* she had been equally thorough, and this was confirmed by Mr. McLellan's smiling remark, "She has left us nothing to conceive or originate — simply to carry on and to execute."

That seemed to me at the time, and seems now, to be a remarkable tribute to the mental and physical ability of a woman of Mrs. Eddy's advanced years!

During the following year, 1909, an opportunity was offered me to associate myself with the Plimpton

Press at Norwood, Massachusetts. This plant was much larger and more modern than the University Press, and the change would ensure the co-operation of an unusually able group of business associates. In view of the personal efforts I had put into the reorganization and development of the University Press during the past eighteen years, I found it difficult even to think of severing my connection, but the advantages, not only to me but to my clients, were so obvious that there really could be only temporary hesitation. I discussed the matter with a few of my customers and found them universally sympathetic. Mr. Stewart was among those whom I approached.

"I think you are undoubtedly making a wise move," he said; "but there is one matter that needs to be taken up. I have among my standing orders an old letter from Mrs. Eddy, dating back, I think, to Dr. Foster-Eddy, instructing the publisher always to leave the manufacture of her books in John Wilson's hands. As you were his successor at the University Press, I have never had occasion to raise any question. If you leave the University Press, are you or is the University Press John Wilson's successor? I have no doubt as to Mrs. Eddy's intentions, but the matter should be settled at this point."

Two days later Mr. Stewart telephoned me: "I have talked with Mrs. Eddy. The shift is all right, of course, but she wants to see you."

This was welcome news. An appointment was made, and I saw Mrs. Eddy for the first time in her new home. It had been five years since my final visit to Pleasant View. Naturally I was prepared for changes. Mrs. Eddy and Pleasant View seemed inseparable to me, and I could not imagine her in any different environment. I walked through the spacious grounds leading to the entrance, and was greeted at the door by one of Mrs. Eddy's secretaries, who immediately ushered me up the stairway to the study where Mrs. Eddy awaited me.

There was but one change I noted — it was the first time she had ever received me sitting down. But the clear voice that greeted me, the bright eyes, and the keen expression of interest belied any thought that her sitting posture was enforced. During our conference she rose with ease — before I could anticipate her — to reach an object on the table. There was another change — in addition to all other personal attributes which were always present, there was an added tranquillity — perhaps serenity is the better word — that crowned them all. Here was a woman approaching the close of an eventful human journey, who really found contentment and happiness awaiting her. There was a moment of silence as all this passed through my mind, which was broken by her greeting. As always there were no words wasted on trivialities. Our conversation started as if there had been no long interruption.

"It is good of you to come," she greeted me. "Of course Mr. Stewart knew, as you know, what my answer would be to his question, but it was right that he should ask me. I sent those instructions to Dr. Foster-Eddy when he was my publisher, as I was afraid he might make a change in printers. When John Wilson placed his mantle upon your shoulders, he himself made you his successor wherever you might be. My old friend put far more than type and printer's ink into the volumes he made, and the lessons you assimilated from him are what I always wish to have incorporated in my books."

Then she proceeded to ask me a series of questions that amazed me — questions one might have expected from an astute businessman addressed to one younger and less experienced: what was the capacity of the Plimpton Press, what was its equipment, how strong was it financially, was the grade of its work comparable with what she had been receiving from the University Press. Of course these were all questions on which I had previously satisfied myself, but she wished specifically to learn the answers.

"You see," she added, as if in explanation, "I am thinking of the future. This change may mean that the Plimpton Press will make my books for many years to come. Mr. Fernald [Josiah E. Fernald, Mrs. Eddy's banker] used a financial expression the last time I saw him which I had never heard before, and

I like it. 'Now is the time,' Mr. Fernald said, 'to consolidate your gains.' That is what I am doing —
consolidating my gains, while I keep on with the
building."

What a wonderful self-analysis of those final fruitful
years!

When I rose to leave, she motioned with her hand
for me to reseat myself. Then came another instance
of that wonderful gift of hers.

"I want you to know," she said, "how sorry I was
to have you disappointed about that grand edition of
Science and Health you had in mind." She referred to
the matter as if it had happened yesterday instead of
nearly two years before. "We gave it careful thought.
The idea pleased me. If and when it is right for this
edition to be made, it will be made."

What other woman, with her mind filled with
matters of her own concern, would have even remembered such an incident so long after it had been considered and settled? What other woman, immersed in
major interests, would have had the kindly thought
to mitigate the disappointment she knew had been
experienced?

Then, as I rose a second time, she added a parting
comment, which was to give me a new idea, and which
served to keep alive the long-cherished dream.

"By the way," she said, "I like your Humanistic
type much better than Mr. Bodoni's!"

Again I thought that this conference would prove to be our last, but again I was happily disappointed. In April, 1910, Mr. Stewart turned over to me a manuscript with the remark: "These are some poems written by Mrs. Eddy at various times during her life. She wishes to have them put into book form — just a small edition for private distribution. I am instructed to hand the manuscript over to you with no further comment than that she would like to have you design the volume for her. I presume you will prepare a dummy to submit for her approval. Let me know when it is ready and I will arrange for you to show it to her."

This was a commission which I accepted with much pleasure. As I have already remarked, with Mrs. Eddy I always presented a single, clearly defined suggestion. I never came in contact with anyone who so definitely knew exactly what she wanted. My procedure, therefore, was always to study the matter in hand from what I thought was her viewpoint, and then submit it for her consideration in a definite form. In the case of the Poems, I remembered her fondness for pink roses, so I instructed my artist to design a cover which included these in the decoration. Then I put in type a few pages of the manuscript in a carefully selected face, and bound the volume in vellum.

My second visit to Chestnut Hill was a happy repetition of the first, but I found Mrs. Eddy in a mood I had never seen before. Instead of her customary poise, she showed a shyness about the publication of her poems quite unlike her usual self-confidence. When I handed her the dummy volume, her face lighted, and she exclaimed with obvious pleasure, "Oh, you have put my pink roses on my poems." She held the dummy in her hands for some minutes before glancing inside.

"These are poems," she said, "which I have written from time to time, ever since I was a girl. Ideas have come to me which I seemed to be able to express better in verse than in prose. I am not sure that they ought to be given the dignity of book publication. I am planning to issue them privately for a few friends."

Then she opened the dummy volume in which I had pasted the pages showing her the type and decoration I suggested. She immediately became deeply absorbed. "How much better this looks in type than in manuscript," she exclaimed.

The first poem I had happened to select for the sample page was "Autumn." She slowly read it aloud but as if to herself, oblivious to all around her. The poem in the original had a descriptive line "Written in childhood in a maple grove." After reading the entire poem aloud, she returned to this line.

"I think the word *girlhood* would be better than *childhood*," she said. And, reaching for a pencil, she made the change in the dummy. Then she read the first verse over again aloud:

What though earth's jewels disappear;
    The turf, whereon I tread,
Ere autumn blanch another year,
    May rest above my head.

She was thoughtful for a moment; then she said,
"I don't like that first line." She drew a pencil through
the words in question and substituted, "Quickly earth's
jewels disappear."

Then she turned to the second poem I had happened to put in type, which was "Meeting of My
Departed Mother and Husband," and the same process
was repeated. The first verse of this poem also attracted
her concentration. In the original manuscript it read:

Joy for thee, happy friend! thy bark is past
The dangerous sea, and safely moored at last —
                    Beyond rough foam.
Soft gales celestial, in sweet music bore —
Mortal emancipate for this far shore —
                    Thee to thy home.

She read this verse aloud twice, emphasizing the
next to the last line, "Mortal emancipate for this far
shore."

Then, after a moment's silence, she said, "*Mortal*
is not the right word." With her pencil she made the
change: "Spirit emancipate for this far shore."

Still with her pencil in hand, she turned to the
inside cover and wrote her name in a firm hand, giving
the dummy her approval. Handing it back to me, she

remarked: "Mr. Stewart is urging me to print also an edition for general distribution. But I am hesitating. Somehow poems seem more personal than prose."

"I hope that you will yield to his persuasion," I remarked.

"Perhaps," she replied, with a smile. "Mr. Stewart will let you know."

Mrs. Eddy's final decision was to issue the book in two styles: a Presentation edition limited to one hundred copies, bound in full vellum, numbered and autographed by the author, and a regular edition of two thousand copies, bound in white cloth, for general distribution. The pink roses were stamped on the covers of both editions. The Presentation edition had a pink ribbon marker, and was enclosed in a box.

This was the last time I saw Mrs. Eddy. I still have among my treasures this actual dummy volume which she autographed, and in which she made the several penciled changes in the text pages to which I have referred. Frequently I take it from the shelf, particularly after I have heard someone speak of Mrs. Eddy in the past tense. This little book may be nothing but paper and binder's board and a few sample pages of type, but it was once encompassed by hands which only eight months later relinquished their hold upon earthly affairs — hands which, guided by the wonderful mind controlling them, had built a mighty structure, proclaiming truth as Mrs. Eddy found it.

Can you wonder that the little volume brings back to me a very vital picture? But when I analyze this, my first reacting thought of Mrs. Eddy is not as a great personality, but rather as a very human woman, whose realness consisted in being always herself, and whose greatness came from her innate genius for understanding others.

When the news came in December, 1910, that Mrs. Eddy's earthly journey had come to a triumphal end, my first reaction was absolute incredulity. Such extraordinary constructive activity as I had personally witnessed during the past eighteen years simply could not be stilled! Nor was it. She had "consolidated her gains" and "kept on building" up to the very end, and in doing so she had merged the vitality of that personal activity to such an extent into the structure she had created that its momentum alone was adequate to carry on to ever greater heights.

PART III

Later Editions
1910 - 1950

Later Editions
1910 - 1950

IT is interesting at this moment of Mrs. Eddy's passing to consider the legacy she bequeathed to humanity, and to assess the position among the world's great personages to which she is so clearly entitled. This is peculiarly difficult because she qualified in so many different ways, and along lines which ordinarily would be considered widely divergent and conflicting.

The world acclaims great authors, but Mrs. Eddy's Science and Health achieved the distinction of outlasting any book ever written by any single author in the history of the world — a book which today, forty years after the passing of its writer, without a single alteration in the text since that day, is in greater demand than at any time during its seventy-five years of existence.

There have been great publishers, but no one among them all ever established so successful an organization founded on such original business methods, including not only books but magazines, and an internationally famous daily newspaper.

There have been great organizers, but I can recall no one of them who so successfully built the structure of a great religious movement while at the same time personally handling or supervising the business background against which it was founded.

There have been great spiritual leaders, but no one among them all has possessed the practical ability to provide by his own efforts the financial security essential to insure success.

There have been great personalities who have inspired the erection of religious edifices which stand as permanent monuments to attest the value of their contributions to the world, but there could be nothing more impressive than the noble group of buildings associated with The Mother Church in Boston, to which must be added the numerous Christian Science churches throughout the world.

Mrs. Eddy was a great executive, and would have been great in any vocation which she had elected to adopt. She chose the most difficult of all. It proved to be full of frustrations, yet each obstacle in being overcome seemed to contribute to this dauntless spirit additional strength with which to meet the next.

It is only by comparing the actual accomplishments made by Mrs. Eddy in varying fields with the achievements of those which warrant comparison that the degree of Mrs. Eddy's greatness can be estimated, but the fullness of it may be best established by the permanence of each achievement after meeting the test of forty years.

It was natural that Mrs. Eddy's passing should have

aroused world-wide conjecture as to its effect on the stability of the Christian Science movement itself. There still remained self-appointed critics who glibly predicted disaster in varying degrees, thus unwittingly paying high tribute to the extraordinarily dynamic force of the Founder up to the very close of her life. Among Christian Scientists themselves it was a summons to greater unification and to greater effort. There could be no doubt whatever, in the minds of those of us who had witnessed the sagacious, farsighted building of the structure, and were familiar with the high caliber of the men Mrs. Eddy had placed in key positions, upon whose shoulders would now fall the responsibility of carrying on, that the work would go on with continuing success.

From the very beginning of the period which followed Mrs. Eddy's passing, those in whom her former authority became vested set about to consolidate the editions already issued, and to plan new editions when, in their opinion, the author's words could be presented to her followers in more acceptable physical form, or reach new fields not as yet explored. During the forty years which have elapsed I have been deeply impressed by the fidelity with which each continuing Board of Directors and Board of Trustees has executed what it has obviously considered to be a sacred trust. During this period I have been gratified to be called into conference several times simply to answer the question,

"What do you think Mrs. Eddy's attitude would be on this?" The extraordinary nature of all this is that with so many changes which have taken place in everything else during these eventful four decades, Mrs. Eddy's successors in control could so scrupulously have followed her original plans, and that these plans were so farsighted as to need no change.

Allison V. Stewart was the last publisher who served directly under Mrs. Eddy, his tenure of office continuing through 1917. They were fruitful years as far as manufacturing went, and the new volumes presented interesting problems. For instance, Wissenschaft und Gesundheit, the German translation of Science and Health, was published in 1912 and was the earliest of the translations of Science and Health into foreign languages.

The first difficulty to overcome in making this volume was the fact that the German language requires more space to say the same thing than the English. The typographic plan called for each German page to face the corresponding English page, which was "frozen" with numbered lines. This required adjusting the type in the German page with varying leads and smaller size so that the page should contain the same subject matter as the English page, even though the copy was expanded in the translation.

Then again there was the matter of the running

heads. The usual practice in bookmaking is to place the title of the volume at the top of the left-hand page and the title of the chapter on the right-hand. In the case of the translations, each page, English and foreign, had to carry both the title of the book and the title of the chapter. All this required considerable experimentation before the final solution was worked out. This is the only case of a double running head I have ever seen. The translation of Science and Health into French, Science et Santé, followed in 1917.

During 1913 some of Mrs. Eddy's addresses and other written messages, not as yet incorporated in book form, were made into the volume called "The First Church of Christ, Scientist, and Miscellany." Mrs. Eddy had prepared the material for this book, and left it for future publication. There was no special typographical problem about the book, the plan being established at this point to keep the new volumes uniform in appearance, so that Mrs. Eddy's books should eventually constitute Mrs. Eddy's "Works."

During this same year, 1913, came the setting of the Concordance to Other Writings. The copy for this was prepared by Albert F. Conant, who, ten years earlier, had compiled the Concordance to Science and Health. I well remember the sensation created at the Plimpton Press when a huge wooden packing case was delivered, having come to us from California. When opened, we found it to contain 3910 cards, on which

Mr. Conant's staff had prepared the most perfect piece of copy for any book which I have ever seen. The problems in manufacturing this book were lighter because of the earlier experience with the Concordance to Science and Health, but a new difficulty was introduced by the fact that this book required references to all of Mrs. Eddy's other writings, instead of to a single volume as was the case in the earlier Concordance.

Scarcely was the new Concordance out of the way than it was decided to reset the Concordance to Science and Health completely. At this time the new edition could be made with a degree of permanence, as the final changes in the textbook had been made. The amount of these changes seems incredible! This is summarized in Mr. Conant's preface to the new edition, in which he says:

> About five thousand new references have been inserted. Of these, nearly sixteen hundred were needed for new words not hitherto indexed; and more than thirty-four hundred were required to index the changes in Science and Health which have been made by its author since the first Concordance was printed. . . . Some idea of the extent of her recent revisions may be gained from the above figures, which thus serve to enhance an appreciative recognition of the indefatigable labors of our Leader in the interests of humanity.

During Mr. Stewart's regime there came a demand for these two Concordances to be issued on Bible paper, in a smaller format. The only way to meet this demand was to photograph these larger pages down to the size desired. Inasmuch as photographic plates are made of softer metal than electrotype plates, the problem of making the desired reduction and still preserving the perfection and clarity of the type required more than ordinary ingenuity.

Mr. Stewart issued the Readers' edition of Science and Health in September, 1914.

The last manufacturing problem I undertook with Mr. Stewart was suggested by the success which had attended the manufacture of the photographic plates for the Standard Leather editions of the Concordances. In 1917, when the United States entered the First World War, there came a demand from the soldiers at the front for some edition of Science and Health which they might carry on their person. To meet this desire a plan was worked out to produce a book, printed on Bible paper and bound in ooze leather, just the size to slip into the pocket of the standard Army khaki shirt. This required reducing the pages of Science and Health to such an extent that not enough margin was left on each page to allow the gripper to hold the plate in place on the press. To overcome this, four pages were photographed together on a single plate, the copy being arranged in such a way as to preserve the narrow margins, and with enough blank metal on two sides to hold the plate firmly on the press. Plans for this work were partly completed when Mr. Stewart resigned as publisher in November, 1917, in order to devote all his time to his duties as Director, to which position he had been appointed in January, 1908.

In October, 1917, the Trustees under the Will of Mary Baker Eddy entered into a contract with the Board of Trustees of The Christian Science Publishing Society to publish Mrs. Eddy's writings, the expectation being that the affairs of producing and distributing the various publications would proceed along the already established lines. The contract had not long been in effect, however, when it became evident that the Trustees of the Publishing Society had plans of their own which did not conform to the desire or expectation of the Trustees under the Will or to Mrs. Eddy's original intentions.

Harry I. Hunt, who had been Mr. Stewart's assistant for over a year, was appointed to serve as "Assistant to the Manager — Printing," under the supervision of the Manager and Board of Trustees of The Christian Science Publishing Society.

Mr. Hunt came from New Jersey, and was well qualified by his earlier advertising experience with the National Cash Register Company; but he found himself seriously handicapped. The details of the manufacture of Mrs. Eddy's writings had previously been left to the publisher, and although Mr. Hunt was specifically in charge of these details, the Board of Trustees of the Publishing Society as then constituted concerned itself with these details to an unusual degree, much to Mr. Hunt's embarrassment. Litigation begun in March, 1919, by the Trustees of the Publishing Society against The Christian Science Board of Directors was then before the Courts of Massachusetts; and when the Trustees under the Will requested of the Trustees of the Publishing Society a cancellation of this contract, the latter refused.

The internal situation at the Publishing House eventually became intolerable, and in March, 1920, Mr. Hunt and several of his associates left. Manufacturing routine practically ceased, and the publication of Mrs. Eddy's books became demoralized for the first and only time. With the authority to place orders for paper, printing, and binding disputed, the regulation reserve stocks ran out, and even the most important titles went into suspense. The lawsuit was finally settled in favor of The Christian Science Board of Directors in November, 1921, but it required nearly a year to restore order. Mr. Hunt was recalled in January, 1922, to assist. The troublesome contract was finally terminated in October, 1922, and in November of that year the Trustees under the Will of Mary Baker Eddy, then the actual publishers of her books, appointed Mr. Hunt as their administrative officer for the publishing work, and gave him the title of Publishers' Agent. A silver lining to the unfortunate experience of the preceding five years was the emphasis the legal decision placed upon Mrs. Eddy's extraordinary foresight in plans for the distant future which were so fundamentally sound that they withstood bitter legal attack.

Mr. Hunt had other unusual situations to meet for the Trustees under the Will, particularly the question of getting Oxford Bible paper from England during the First World War. He had been forehanded in ordering advance stock, but there were two or three instances where the shipments from England were delayed, which made slight irregularities in maintaining the required stock. In spite of the paper famine which existed in this country during this period, his foresight had been sufficient to provide adequate paper for his necessities in the case of the clothbound books.

An entirely new responsibility was placed upon the office of the publisher in 1920, which had to do with the binding of the limp leather copies of Science and Health and other titles. Mrs. Eddy had been wise in placing the order for the leather binding at the very beginning in the hands of Dudley and Hodge, who were then located in the Cathedral Building on Franklin Street in Boston. Later they moved to Washington Street, opposite the Old South Church. Limp leather binding such as was required for Science and Health was an art little practiced in this country. Mr. Hodge, however, was an English-trained workman, who had learned his trade with the Oxford Bible people in England. He knew his business thoroughly, and exercised his knowledge in a constructive way in establishing from the earliest days the high quality of binding which has always been characteristic of the limp leather-bound volumes of Mrs. Eddy's writings.

At first every process associated with the binding was executed by hand. Up to 1900 one woman and one man formed a sufficient staff to fill orders for the textbook in morocco bindings. By the time Mr. Hunt assumed office, however, the work required 135 workers, and the demand was constantly growing. In 1920, therefore, The Christian Science Publishing Society purchased the Dudley and Hodge bindery, and for a time operated the plant in the dingy Washington Street headquarters. In March, 1922, the bindery was removed to more commodious quarters at 88 St. Stephen Street, not far from the Publishing House itself.

The practical running of the plant was handled by the experienced personnel Dudley and Hodge had established, but the oversight became a function of the office of Publishers' Agent. This placed a still further responsibility on Mr. Hunt, although he had indirectly borne a part of it for some time, owing to the fact that it was the practice for the Publishers to purchase and supply to Dudley and Hodge the skins required for the binding. This material was provided by goats bred in India, and the skins had to be sent from India to London to be dyed and processed, and then from London to Boston, their final destination.

I remember an interesting story Mr. Hunt told me at this time. Toward the end of World War I, with materials on hand sufficient for perhaps six months, the supply suddenly failed, and no more India goatskins could be secured. Mr. Hunt promptly started experiments for substituting sheepskins for goatskins, but just before the question of substitution had to be settled, a ship loaded with goatskins arrived from China, the use of which tided over the gap until it was possible again to secure goatskins from India.

Mr. Hunt was much interested when he learned the cause of the sudden stoppage. It seems that the natives of India are familiar only with the silver rupee as money. During World War I silver rupees were used to pay the Indian troops sent to Egypt and Gallipoli, which required all the silver money in the country. When the Indian farmers, therefore, offered their goatskins for sale at the local fairs, and were offered paper money for them instead of silver, they refused to accept it. As soon as silver coinage in India was resumed, the Indian goatskins again came plentifully into the market.

The leather bindery, under the title of the Publishers' Book Bindery, was continued under the direction of the Publishers' Agent until 1938, at which time the entire plant was taken over by private interests. The machinery was moved to Cambridge, and the business continued without interruption. The quality of work which has always been associated with the limp leather binding of Mrs. Eddy's works is seldom equaled and never surpassed, even in the finest Bibles the world produces.

In December, 1924, Science and Health appeared in Braille. This was not the first of Mrs. Eddy's writings to be thus translated into raised print for the blind, "Rudimental Divine Science" having been published in February, 1906, and "Unity of Good" in March, 1923. This first issue of Science and Health was five hundred copies (twenty-five hundred books, five books to the set), and was the largest single edition of any book ever printed in Braille at one time, according to the Braille Institute of America. Other titles to be thus treated later were "Retrospection and Introspection" (1930), Church Manual (1936), and Seven Poems (1936).

The most important new publication of the Trustees under the Will while Mr. Hunt held office was Prose Works (1925). In this single volume everything Mrs. Eddy had written aside from Science and Health was included except the Church Manual, her Poems, and "Christ and Christmas." The popularity of Prose Works has exceeded all other titles except Science and Health and the Church Manual. During this same year the Half-century Edition commemorated the fiftieth celebration of the publication of the first edition of Science and Health.

During 1928 through 1936 "Rudimental Divine Science" was translated into Danish, Dutch, French, German, Norwegian, Swedish, Czech, Spanish, and Russian. "Retrospection and Introspection," during 1932–1934, was also translated into all the above languages except Czech, Spanish, and Russian. Seven Messages, in English, appeared in 1935. The year 1936 was a productive one, its most important event being the publication of Science and Health in the Sunday School edition, less attractive than the Library edition, but sold at a lower price. As against this, the Trustees under the Will issued the De Luxe edition of the textbook, in the most elaborate format until the Subscription Edition. Finding that some Christian Scientists considered the original large size of "Christ and Christmas" difficult to hold, I was asked to have the plates of the illustrations reduced and to reset the verses, combining this title with Mrs. Eddy's Poems in one volume. This was issued only in leather binding at that time. The Cleartype edition of Science and Health appeared in 1936.

Mr. Hunt retired in 1939 in order to devote all his time to the practice of Christian Science.

Hudson C. Burr became Mr. Hunt's successor in August, 1939. He was a native of Plainfield, New

Jersey, and a graduate of Brown University, where he received his degree in electrical engineering. During World War I he served as a flying engineer officer, and after the war was engaged in the advertising business, subsequently becoming manager of national advertising for *The Christian Science Monitor*.

When he became Publishers' Agent, Mr. Burr brought new vitality to a well-established business and a knowledge of the value of publicity. His experience in the *Monitor's* advertising department had convinced him of its paramount importance, and under the Trustees' direction he broadened and modernized the advertising of Mrs. Eddy's works in the Christian Science publications.

An important responsibility that fell on him in 1941 was the complete resetting of all Mrs. Eddy's books — the first time a change had been made since the edition I manufactured for Mrs. Eddy herself in 1902. The Trustees under the Will had decided that the time had come to give to the volumes a more modern touch, and Mr. Burr asked me to suggest such changes as I felt would accomplish this result. Ever mindful of Mrs. Eddy's personal injunction, given years before, that "the page of a familiar book was like the face of an old friend," I made as few changes as possible in bringing the typography up to modern requirements. The most notable variation is to be found in the treatment of the chapter heads and the running heads, mostly minor matters, and yet important in themselves. Who was it said, "Trifles make perfection, but perfection is no trifle"?

In view of the dangers of war, it was decided at this time to make three sets of molder plates, and to store these in different parts of the country to reduce the risk of destruction by bombing or fire.

The important part played by Mr. Burr in the production of the Subscription Edition of Science and Health is fully told in the following section of this book. I cannot overstate my appreciation of his understanding co-operation and his contagious enthusiasm.

In September, 1942, Mr. Burr resigned his position as Publishers' Agent to accept appointment as a Trustee of The Christian Science Publishing Society.

Alfred Pittman, of Chicago, Illinois, succeeded Mr. Burr as Publishers' Agent. He is a native of St. Joseph, Missouri, and a graduate of William Jewell College in that state. Later he continued his studies in England under a scholarship from the American Association for International Conciliation, and also at Harvard University. Prior to his appointment as Publishers' Agent he had served on the editorial staff of *The Christian Science Monitor*, the *Kansas City Star*, and on the magazines *System* and *Factory*. In 1940, after several years devoted to the public practice of Christian Science, Mr. Pittman was elected an associate editor of *The Christian Science Journal, Sentinel,* and *Herald.* With this background, he brought a literary atmosphere to his new office of Publishers' Agent, to which he was elected in October, 1942.

Mr. Pittman was in hearty sympathy with Mr. Burr's efforts to modernize the typography of Mrs. Eddy's books, and extended this effort to the binding. Such anachronisms as round corners and marbled edges were eliminated, and a handsome Royal blue cloth replaced the previous standardized black of the Library editions and the blue and brown of the Sunday School edition.

Special experiments were made to secure the exact shade of blue which the fifteenth-century artists mixed for their own palettes, and at the same time to secure a color that would not fade.

This question of color recalls my continuing surprise that from the beginning Mrs. Eddy permitted such a wide variation in the cloth bindings of Science and Health. At various times the volume appeared in brown, purple, black, green, blue, and even red. My only explanation is that her mind was so concentrated upon the meticulous presentation of her thought in the printed page, that she was content to leave the clothing of the book to the taste of her publisher or the convenience of the binder. The earliest attempt at standardization was made by Mr. Hunt and completed by Mr. Pittman.

During this period, in co-operation with branch churches and societies, the Trustees under the Will expanded their plans for greater publicity into a nation-wide advertising campaign in secular newspapers, supplementing this by issuing a Special Cloth edition of Science and Health in 1946, which became available to the public through the regular bookstores. This advertising campaign, which started in sixteen of the larger American cities, was expanded in 1945 to thirty cities, and during the following year ten more were added, including four overseas English-speaking areas.

Increasing difficulties in getting Oxford Bible paper from England, and rumbling of approaching war, led me, with Mr. Pittman's co-operation, to a determined effort to stimulate the manufacture of a comparable Bible paper in the United States. After many disappointing experiments, an admirable sheet was developed, and became available only a few weeks before World War II completely cut off the English supply.

In March, 1947, Mr. Pittman resigned as Publishers' Agent to accept his election to The Christian Science Board of Directors.

With Mr. Pittman's resignation, Hudson C. Burr was reappointed Publishers' Agent, but this second term lasted only a little over two years, owing to his passing in April, 1949. These two years, however, were full of activity. Ciencia y Salud, the Spanish translation of Science and Health, was pushed through to completion in April, 1947, and Vetenskap och Hälsa, the Swedish translation, followed in April, 1948. These were the first translations to appear printed on Bible paper, and bound in cloth. In 1948 the Trustees under the Will issued the small edition of "Christ and Christmas," combined with Poems, in cloth binding. This had been originally published in 1936, but in leather binding only. The new issue made it possible to secure all Mrs. Eddy's writings in clothbound volumes, uniform in size and binding. During this period the growing development of the national publicity was consolidated by the organization of the Service and Sales Department as a definite function of the Publishers' Agent. While Mr. Burr served, the Students' edition of Science and Health, which had been planned originally in Mr. Pittman's time, to replace the Sunday School edition, was introduced.

The vacancy caused by Mr. Burr's passing in April, 1949, was filled by Horace J. Carver, the present incumbent. He was born in Racine, Wisconsin. After receiving his degree from the University of Wisconsin, he became sales manager of a textile company in the Middle West, and later removed to New York to become vice president of an advertising research organization, ultimately resigning this work in order to become a Christian Science practitioner. Mr. Carver was called

to Boston to serve as manager of the new Service and
Sales Department at the office of the Publishers' Agent,
a position which he was filling at the time of Mr. Burr's
passing. He became Mr. Burr's natural successor, being ·
appointed to that position in April, 1949.

During his tenure of office he has made a valuable
contribution by arranging for the issuance of a little
volume entitled "What Christmas Means to Me," in
which are gathered together expressions which concern
Christmas selected from Mrs. Eddy's writings.

French and German cloth pocket editions of the
textbook printed on Bible paper were released to the
Reading Rooms, and Prose Works was issued in
cloth binding. Another significant publication during
Mr. Carver's regime is the beautiful Seventy-fifth
Anniversary Edition, commemorating the first publication of Science and Health. For this the text was
completely reset in a larger type. It is bound in leather
and also in cloth.

Thus during the past sixty years there have been
four publishers and four Publishers' Agents, the latter
serving under the Trustees under the Will, with
responsibility to further the presentation of Mrs. Eddy's
works. These men have been of widely different types
with equally different training, and have come from
various parts of the country; but with the exception
of the first two publishers, who served before Mrs.

Eddy was able firmly to establish basic lines of operation, each one has distinctly contributed to the successful development of the definite plan conceived and laid down by Mrs. Eddy herself. The ease with which each has taken over his predecessor's work, and the success with which he has assimilated his responsibility are evidence of the basic soundness of that original plan, which could only be conceived by a great executive.

During all these years there has been but one unvarying injunction placed upon the printer, "Make no change unless such change produces a finer book." The individuals responsible for the publication of Mrs. Eddy's writings have painstakingly studied the needs of Christian Scientists all over the world, and have been tireless in striving to present the message conveyed through these writings in such a way as to meet every possible desire and convenience.

It is an amazing record of loyalty, ability, and achievement.

PART IV

The Subscription Edition of Science and Health

1939 - 1941

The Subscription Edition of Science and Health was issued in June, 1941, in a limited edition of one thousand copies. In format, it is a Super Royal Quarto, 10 by 14 inches, 725 pages, set in Laurentian type, especially revised and cut for this volume. It is printed in red and black on pure linen-rag, handmade paper, bulking three inches. The binding is in full imported morocco, blind stamped. Each copy is enclosed in a cloth-covered, fleece-lined wooden box. The edition was oversubscribed before publication.

The Subscription Edition of Science and Health

1939 - 1941

THE production of the Subscription Edition of
Science and Health is an epic in the history of
American bookmaking, and becomes an integral
part of this story because whatever later use may be
made of the Laurentian type, this design will always
be associated with that volume. I call it an epic with
no measure of self-praise, but as an historical fact. I
was but the motivating force, and without the extraordinarily loyal and enthusiastic co-operation of everyone
along the line from start to finish, that motivation
would never have accomplished the results it did.

Beginning with the designing of the type, there were
Dr. Guido Biagi, Prefect of the Laurentian Library at
Florence, and Monsignor Ceriani, Prefect of the Ambrosian Library at Milan. These distinguished masters of
learning gave generously of their time and knowledge
in searching out the finest examples of the work of
the humanistic scribes, and submitting them to me to
serve as models. In London there were Sir Sidney
Colvin and Alfred W. Pollard — respectively heads of

the Departments of Engraving and of the Printed Book at the British Museum — who went over my drawings with me and made important technical suggestions. At home there was Charles Eliot Norton, my old professor of Art at Harvard University, who gave encouragement by his enthusiastic approval. There were Sir John Murray IV, the famous London publisher, and John Murray Brown of the equally famous Boston firm of Little, Brown & Company, who promptly offered to publish in Great Britain and America the series of Humanistic volumes I had tentatively planned to issue in my new type. There was Joseph W. Phinney, head of the American Type Founders Company, who, when my drawings were finally completed, placed his most skillful punch cutter at my disposal.

And behind all this far-flung activity was the casual remark made by Mrs. Eddy to an enthusiastic youngster more than forty years before at Pleasant View, "If one has beauty in himself, he can put beauty into anything," which was the sowing of the seed that in flowering set everything in motion!

All this relates to the hand type which I first designed and called "Humanistic." It was thirty years later that I revised the letters, and had the font recut to adapt itself to a typesetting machine, as was necessary to produce the Subscription Edition of Science and Health. This I rechristened "Laurentian" in recognition of the part the Laurentian Library of Florence,

Italy, had played in its creation. Thus the story of the Laurentian type is identical with the Humanistic face up to the point of its recutting for machine. Now we must retrace our steps.

Back in Dr. Biagi's sanctum we are glancing over the pages of Sinibaldi's "Virgil," and other volumes handwritten by the humanistic scribes. Listen to what the genial Doctor is telling us of their history, which supplies the necessary background to our type:

"The humanistic movement," he is saying, "dates back to the thirteenth century. It was the forerunner and the essence of the Renaissance, being in reality a revolt against the barrenness of medievalism. Until then, intellectual life had been confined on all sides by ignorance, superstition, and tradition, but Petrarch and his enthusiastic band of humanists advanced a claim for the mental freedom of man, and for the complete development of his being. In making this claim, they demanded nothing less than the recognition of the rich humanities of Greece and Rome, which had been proscribed. If their claim had been postponed another half century, the actual manuscripts of many of the present standard classics would have been lost to the world through neglect or deliberate destruction."

Then came the invention of printing. At first the patrons of the arts, who comprised the wealthy, cultured class which ruled Italy, treated it with indifference and contempt. A book manufactured by machine to them was unworthy of notice. But the man in the street took notice. This new invention was a duplication of the handwritten volumes at a price he could pay, and the enthusiasm was so universal that the patrons began to be alarmed. Libraries in those days were symbols of wealth, and through wealth and the opportunity to learn came power. If the masses once gained an opportunity to read, criticism, which had remained the monopoly of the scholars, would come into the hands of the people, and when the masses once learned self-reliance from this new intellectual development, they could attack dogma and political oppression.

There was another, less selfish reason for this opposition. To produce a volume by mechanical means seemed to these true booklovers to be an insult to the thought contained between its covers. To them the magnificent illuminated volumes were not merely examples of the decorator's art, but a tangible tribute paid by these highly educated nobles to the thought conveyed. To them, the thought was a jewel, and they considered this jewel more precious than any costly gem. In their own libraries they recognized its value by employing the most accomplished scribes to write out the thought on parchment; they embellished this by illuminated miniatures and decoration, executed by the most famous artists; they protected the written pages with bindings in which, in some instances, gold, silver, and jewels were actually inlaid. This was their expression of affection and respect.

But all their effort to silence the demand from the people for the printed book was in vain. Now thoroughly alarmed, the rulers turned to their last weapon —ridicule. They would show the people what a miserable thing a printed book really was! To demonstrate this, orders were given to the scribes as never before, with the command that the letters were "to be shaped with careful study of their proportions, each to be a specimen of good taste and perfect execution." In short, the artist-scribes were instructed to produce the most beautiful handwritten volumes ever seen. Under the spur of this demand the art of handlettering reached its highest point, and the Sinibaldi "Virgil" we have just examined in Dr. Biagi's sanctum is one of the actual books thus produced, the patron being the House of Medici.

Now we have reached the point where I became especially intrigued. These are the notes I made at that time:

The first type cut by Gutenberg was based upon the Gothic handlettering of his period. This design was appropriate to ecclesiastical books like the Gutenberg Bible, but entirely inappropriate for classical works. When, therefore, Sweynheim and Pannartz in Subiaco undertook to print Cicero's Letters, they designed the first roman type face in existence, and based it upon the best roman handletter of their period.

This roman type of Sweynheim and Pannartz was revised by John of Spires, and was later perfected by Nicolas Jenson in Venice.

The Jenson roman face was used as a basis for various famous private types — William Morris' Golden type, Emery Walker's Doves type, and Bruce Rogers' Centaur type.

It is to be noted that the most famous private types in existence have been based upon a *type* model rather than on a hand letter. Still more important, handlettering as an art reached its highest point of perfection in the work of these humanistic scribes *after* the design of the Jenson roman type face, based upon an earlier and inferior hand letter. This little period at the close of the fifteenth century, during which the humanistic scribes produced a limited number of manuscript volumes, had been entirely overlooked by all type designers. Yet the humanistic design is recognized by all authorities as handlettering in its most beautiful form.

When I exclaimed, "Why has this never been taken as the basis of a type?" Dr. Biagi replied, "This, my friend, is your opportunity." The die was cast and my adventure was under way.

Stay with me during the following weeks while I was seeking the fascinating path suggested by Dr. Biagi's remarks. In studying the early fonts of type, I found them deliberate counterfeits of the best existing forms of handlettering which the scribes employed at that time. The scribe, forming his letters with a free hand, produced them inevitably with certain irregularities. This variation is agreeable to the eye in a manuscript, but when an imperfect letter is cut in metal, and repeats the irregularities several times upon the same page, the result is not so pleasing. Nicolas Jenson, who did such wonderful printing at Venice during the last quarter of the fifteenth century, was the first to appreciate this, and in cutting his famous roman type, he departed from the common practice above described by making each letter not as it actually appeared but as he was convinced the scribe intended to make it. As a result, the Jenson type has been taken as the basis of the best standard roman fonts even down to the present time, and has also proved the inspiration for the distinctive type faces already mentioned. All these designs, however, depart distinctly from the Jenson model, and express the individual originality of the artist.

The more I studied the humanistic letters, the less I felt inclined to put myself into the design. By a happy chance I had stumbled upon a little period in the history of bookmaking where handlettering had been carried to the highest point of perfection ever attained. Why not devote my efforts to applying the same principle adopted by Nicolas Jenson: namely, to correct the irregularities, and reproduce each letter not as actually written but as I was convinced the scribe intended it to be, thus removing the objectionable irregularities but retaining the original beauty of the design itself? If the world recognized these letters to represent handlettering at its highest point of perfection, it seemed presumptuous for anyone to do more than translate the beauty of the scribe's work into the rigid requirements of metal.

Thus it was that at first I confined myself to a study of the humanistic volumes in the Laurentian Library, selecting examples that seemed to be best suited as final models for the various letters. These I had photographed. Out of fifty examples, perhaps a half dozen would be almost identical, and from this composite result I learned the exact design which the scribe had endeavored to repeat. Then the idea came to me that perhaps the pleasing variations which distinguish a manuscript from a printed volume might be retained if I introduced the novelty of making variants for certain of the often-repeated letters. This would preserve the individuality of the handlettering but still keep my design within the rigid limitations of type. I therefore made separate drawings of such letters as a, e, h, m, and n. When put in use, the compositor was taught to produce the variation as he thought his hand might change if he were the scribe himself.

When I had exhausted the humanistic volumes at the Laurentian Library, I went on to Milan and the Ambrosian Library, with a letter from Dr. Biagi addressed to Monsignor Ceriani, the Prefect, explaining the work upon which I was engaged, and suggesting his co-operation. Ceriani was a very old man at that time. He was tall and slight, and I remember thinking when I first saw him that his skin, in color and texture, resembled the very parchment of the volumes he handled with such deep affection. No one could more perfectly personify the ancient learning in which he was so deeply steeped. The aged Librarian did not hesitate to place at my disposal all the humanistic volumes in the library of which he was custodian. He could hardly have been more keenly interested in my quest.

And so, after discussing the drawings and the photostats in London with Sir John Murray, Sir Sidney Colvin, and Sir Emery Walker, I sailed for America, full of enthusiasm to put the wheels in motion to carry the adventure on to completion. The skilled punch cutter assigned to me by Mr. Phinney of the American Type Founders Company proved to be extremely co-operative, and I turned everything over to him while I again picked up the routine details of affairs at the University Press, among which was the important resetting of the 1902 edition of Science and Health.

The cutting of the punches proved a slow and laborious operation. Then came the testing of the first types cut, the correction of minor imperfections, the final selection of the paper, and the actual manufacture, requiring the best part of four years. But in 1905, the "Triumphs of Petrarch," the first volume ever to be printed in Humanistic type, became an accomplished fact, being issued simultaneously in England and America. The acclaim which was given to the new type was gratifying, and is recorded here as the verdict of experts regarding the type face which will always be associated with the Subscription Edition of Science and Health.

The critic in the *Boston Transcript* wrote:

While avoiding the slight irregularities of manuscript lettering which would have proved unpleasant in print, the charming freedom from cut and dried forms which marks the handwritten page and is so distinctly absent from the usual book page, is in the new type secured by the use of several variant designs for the same letter. In obedience again to the manuscript model, the font is cut upon a principle quite opposed to the prevailing method; namely, the ascending letters such as b and h are short and the descending letters such as y and g are long. Moreover these ascending and descending lines protrude beyond the foundation body of the type so that they may extend into the spaces of the preceding and following lines with a considerable gain in harmony. All the letters have a remarkable way of preserving their individual distinction when considered one by one, yet sinking this and becoming parts of a word which seems as complete in itself as a logotype. A comparison of this Humanistic type with other faces shows that it possesses an unusual legibility and a color value quite distinct because of the harmony which exists between the heavy and the hair lines. The entire impression produced by a page of Humanistic type is peculiarly effective in grace and elegance, and the combination of artistic distinction and mechanical adequacy is quite rare in the annals of printing.

The Connoisseur, the leading art magazine in London, had this to say:

There is a curious balance in harmony — an absence of the mechanical appearance inherent in printed type, owing to the variations in certain letters, a difference discernible enough to be seen in detail but quite sufficient to be appreciated in the page. Yet in the securing of this important artistic effect the remarkable legibility of the fount is in no way affected or impaired, and there is a pleasant sense of novelty in our being introduced, as it were, to the humanistic scribes, who, in writing out these fine manuscripts after the introduction of printing, have been put on their mettle to bring their art to its highest development . . . indeed the volume is one of the noblest which has issued from the Press in recent years, and marks a new departure in printed books.

Charles Eliot Norton in a magazine article enlarged on what he wrote me when he first saw my drawings:

An interesting and novel experiment is now making at the University Press in Cambridge in having recourse for a new font of type, not to old fonts as models but to the finest of written manuscripts. There can be little question that the experiment is in the right direction. Most modern type lacks freshness and individuality, but the Humanistic font shows its contrast to the familiar dry mechanical type. There is attractive freedom and unusual grace in its lines derived immediately from the manuscript model but adapted to the necessary requirements of print.

The favorable reception given to the new design by critics and booklovers naturally pleased me, the climax coming when I received word that a jury of artists, appointed by the Italian Government to select a type for a magnificent definitive edition of Dante, had settled upon the Humanistic as their choice, this great work to be printed by Bertieri in Milan; yet never once during this period had the type suggested itself in connection with Science and Health. Had my first proposal of a "sumptuous" edition in 1900 found favor, my mind might have associated my first acquaintance with the Humanistic letters with my ambitious dream — but that dream had definitely been put aside. It would have been natural for me to think of the type instead of Bodoni's in my proposal of 1908, but at that time my contracts with John Murray and Little, Brown & Company called for its exclusive use in the Humanistic series. The first real idea of selecting the type for a "sumptuous" edition of Science and Health came from Mrs. Eddy herself, when in 1910 she so unexpectedly remarked, "I like your Humanistic type better than Mr. Bodoni's." Then I became overwhelmed by the conviction that if that "right" time, to which Mrs. Eddy had relegated the whole proposition, ever came, the distinctive edition of Science and Health should be set in no other type than the one I had created under her unwitting supervision. So I settled down to await the "right" time, still nearly thirty years distant!

The intervening years were full of other and important problems, chief among which was changing my base of operations from the University Press to the Plimpton Press, which required a long but completely satisfactory readjustment. But the passage of time did not eliminate my strong desire to produce Science and Health in what I felt more and more to be a fitting dress. In 1929, I received from the Lanston Monotype Company a beautiful brochure showing what they had accomplished in making a specially designed type adaptable for a typesetting machine. It was called the Pastonchi type, and had been designed and cut for service in an edition of Italian classics. Up to this time typesetting machines had contented themselves with making available to book manufacturers only the more orthodox standard book faces, but here was a definite departure. The long-suppressed urge was stimulated. If the special face shown in the brochure could be made available for machine composition, why not the Humanistic? A few days later I was in Philadelphia at the office of the Lanston Monotype Machine Company discussing the problem with Mr. Sol Hess, head of the Art Department. Before the matter I had so close at heart could again be taken up with The

Christian Science Board of Directors, I must assure myself of the possibility of adapting the type. Suppose we let Mr. Hess take up the story at this point:

Mr. Orcutt presented an unusual and fascinating problem — certainly one which held promise of romance and allure. Many types of our present day and age are of a somewhat rigid and mechanical cut. Here we were faced with an entirely different proposition. Basically it was not a type face at all, but handdrawn lettering representative of the finest forms found in the humanistic volumes of fifteenth-century Italy. Was it possible to make a faithful copy of Mr. Orcutt's design? If so, could type then be cast in justified lines so that the final result would emulate the original manuscript pages? Could the color, the height, the close fitting, the length of ascending and descending parts, and other details of design be retained? Was the monotype die case flexible enough to accommodate each and every character without loss of shape or subtlety of design?

It was obvious that the answer to these questions was of paramount importance. . . . The lettering of pages of centuries ago by means of a pen, stylus, or quill was one medium; imitating those pages by means of a modern mechanical device was another. The first step was to make a careful study of the designs in an attempt to maintain the characters in their authentic shape. Indeed to get the feel of the design it was almost necessary to transport oneself mentally to Italy, to be immersed in that fine atmosphere of antiquity and highly artistic achievement. (*Inland Printer*, July, 1941.)

I was fortunate in gaining the co-operation of a

kindred spirit. There were serious obstacles which at first caused Mr. Hess to question the practical feasibility of accomplishing our purpose. But his experience, artistic understanding, and innate genius for solving problems associated with type combined in producing his final verdict that the type could be cut.

All this resulted in bringing back the old enthusiasm. Assured that my type could be produced, which eliminated the question of hand type and hand compositors, my next step was the production of sample pages and a dummy volume, prepared in such a way as to give tangible expression to what I had held captive in my mind for all these years. I therefore had several pages of Science and Health set in the Humanistic hand type. It required weeks to secure a page which would carry the original text of Science and Health line for line and word for word in this larger size. Even these early sample pages showed me the problems I would have to overcome if, as, and when we ever came to setting the whole book in the new type. But at least the sample pages faithfully showed the beauty which might be attached to the text.

A dummy volume was then made up of blank handmade paper, and bound in full morocco, with stamping to give a suggestion of the proposed outward appearance of the book, while the sample pages, proved in red and black and pasted on the inside, gave a similar preview of the text matter. All this was done before I even mentioned the matter to anyone associated with the Trustees under the Will of Mary Baker Eddy. Satisfied at last that my dummy volume expressed my ideas, I took it in to Mr. Hunt, who was at that time Publishers' Agent, and, with the book before us, I outlined what I had in mind. Mr. Hunt was interested, but at first not enthusiastic. He felt that the Trustees would consider it too great an undertaking, but he would be glad to have the dummy volume left with him for later consideration.

From time to time reference was made to the volume, but five years passed by before anything further was done about it. At that time Hudson C. Burr, who later was to be appointed Mr. Hunt's successor as Publishers' Agent, was being trained for his position by Mr. Hunt. One of the things he stumbled against was this dummy volume, and Mr. Hunt suggested that he talk it over with me. Mr. Burr was a younger man, interested in beautiful things, and the idea of a "sumptuous" edition of Science and Health appealed to him strongly. From that moment I had a strong ally in the office of the Publishers' Agent, and when Mr. Burr came fully in charge definite plans were discussed between us for presenting the whole problem to the Trustees under the Will of Mary Baker Eddy.

A dramatic incident occurred while this dummy volume was resting on Mr. Burr's desk awaiting the opportune moment for him to present the proposition to the Trustees. He and I were talking about an entirely different matter when William P. McKenzie, then a member of the Board of Directors, with whom I had worked out the problems associated with the 1902 edition of Science and Health, was announced. Scarcely had he entered the office than his eye fell upon the dummy.

"Look at it," Mr. Burr suggested, smiling.

Mr. McKenzie glanced at the stamped cover, then opened to the printed sample pages within. The moment his eye took in the whole volume, he exclaimed, "That type! That type! How beautiful! If Mrs. Eddy could only see this." There were tears in his eyes as he spoke.

This accidental preview opened the way at last for an early consideration of the proposition by the Trustees. After Mr. Burr's original presentation, the Trustees graciously invited me to appear before them and to tell my story firsthand. The only condition that I made, if the volume was to be issued at all, was that there should be no limit placed upon the expense. Everything about the book, workmanship and materials, must be fashioned along the lines adopted by the old-time artist printers who made quality their only guide. This condition, instead of being an obstacle, appealed to the Trustees. After due deliberation, I was advised by Mr. Burr that they had approved the suggestion, and I was asked to proceed definitely with the work. It was a thrilling moment, after waiting thirty-eight years, to have this opportunity placed before me to create this edition of Science and Health along the lines which I believed Mrs. Eddy would have selected were she still able to pass on the plan. The only flaw in my gratification was the fact that the book could not have been produced during her lifetime.

The commission for this work was given me on August 15, 1939. I immediately cabled orders to England for the paper and to India for the leather. Then the plan seemed hopelessly postponed! England declared war on Germany on September 1, 1939. The clients of the Plimpton Press, naturally wishing to mark time, were canceling or postponing their orders. I heard nothing further from Mr. Burr in regard to the contract for this Subscription Edition of Science and Health. As I was making considerable commitments for the Trustees in the matter of paper and leather, I felt I must have definite advice, so I asked Mr. Burr to take the matter up with the Trustees. The response was immediate:

"Inasmuch as Christian Science is based upon the understanding that good will conquer evil, it seems to us that to cancel or to postpone the order for the Subscription Edition of Science and Health would be stultifying. The book is needed now more than ever. Please proceed."

I am very fond of quoting this incident as an evidence of the absolute consistency which I have found during all these years in my relations with the Trustees under the Will and the Trustees of the Publishing Society.

Now that the order was actually confirmed, the recutting of the revised Humanistic type into what was to be known as the Laurentian face was begun. We had previously cut a few trial characters, particularly those which threatened to prove more troublesome than others, such as the capitals E, O, and S, and the lower case d, e, g, and n. After the matrices were completed, and the types cast, certain words were set up and tried out with varying impressions on different kinds of paper. These trials, after a few minor changes, demonstrated that the pen-drawn "feel" of the humanistic lettering of the fifteenth century could actually be retained and reproduced in rigid, movable, metal type.

Mr. Hess comments upon this stage as follows:

Then our absorbing adventure was fairly launched. Subsequent developments proved it to be one of the most delightful I have undertaken. Careful micrometer measurements were made of each type character to the accuracy of one ten-thousandth part of an inch. After these measurements were completed, a tentative matrix case arrangement was drawn up. Extra designs of the lower case a, e, h, m, and n were furnished. This innovation was introduced to preserve the individuality of handlettering. All these extra characters were included in the die case. We were surprised to find the entire project held much promise because the original well proportioned letter-shapes and the close fitting could be retained with little or practically no change.

The matrices were designed to take care of certain individual letter characteristics such as the long, sweeping tail of the caps Q, R, and lower case y. As in the original version, the monotype characters were fitted exceedingly close, so close that in some cases the letters almost bumped. The original length of ascenders and unusually long descenders was retained. Particular care was given to the finish of the fine, sharp hairlines and serifs so as to simulate as closely as possible the nibs of a pen — that is, a pen-drawn effect. (*Inland Printer*, July, 1941.)

While the cutting of the type was under way I worked out the human problem as it was to affect the use of this type. The keyboard operators at the Plimpton Press were all skillful workmen, but I wanted more than a workman. I wanted a skilled operator who guided his fingers not only with the head but from the heart, so that the humanistic "feel" could be transmitted to the work itself. Among these keyboard operators was a young woman who seemed particularly to possess the characteristic I sought. So, while waiting for the type, I undertook to give her a course in humanism, which would eventually find expression at the tips of her fingers. I showed her specimens of the work of the humanistic scribes; I explained the significance of the Humanistic movement as I have tried to do in this chapter. I told her that the variants of the various letters were to be used sparingly, only when she felt that the hand of the letterer would have found relief in making the slight change. Her enthusiasm gave me great confidence, which was amply justified when the matrices actually were received and put into operation.

The text of Science and Health itself offers unusual problems to be overcome by the ingenuity of the compositor. It will be remembered that Mrs. Eddy continued to make verbal alterations in the text even after the 1902 edition, in which, for the first time, the lines were numbered; the Concordance had since been made, so it had been imperative to make these changes without disturbing the reference numbers. If a word substituted happened to have more letters, it naturally overcrowded the line, or if fewer letters, it left the line too widely spaced. Even in the smaller size type employed in the regular editions, all the ingenuity of the typesetter and the electrotyper was required to secure satisfactory results. When, however, the same page is set in a larger face type, like the Laurentian, the problem becomes even more serious than before. The expedient we adopted in the actual work was to reset the widely spaced lines in a narrower measure, which improved spacing between the words, and these lines were then adjusted so that, when recast, they made lines full width, imperceptibly increasing the size of each character. The closely spaced lines, on the other hand, were rerun with each piece of type slightly shaved, which reduced the line to its proper width. In one instance the type was fattened and in the other shaved.

With the mechanical difficulties provided for, the operator at the keyboard was cautioned to approach her undertaking in the same spirit as a humanistic scribe when he seated himself before a piece of parchment. She was warned against trying to maintain speed, and admonished to keep her thoughts carefully centered upon accuracy not only in using the characters themselves but in spacing the words in each line. During the months required to put the whole of the text of Science and Health into type, I was delighted to find that the enthusiasm of this young woman operator increased rather than diminished. I had succeeded in making her feel that she was not setting type but was building a typographic monument, and the result of it all became quite apparent when the work was finally completed. After the proofreaders had finished with the careful examination of the accuracy, I myself went over every word, letter by letter, making changes in the spacing or in the use of the variant wherever I felt it would improve the appearance of the page. It was a laborious undertaking for all concerned, but there was something about it which made the labor a joy instead of just a piece of work to be done.

While the typesetting was in progress in 1940, I was encountering my first war hazard as applied to the paper. The selection of the paper called for the best pure linen, all rag, handmade paper the world could produce. At Eynsford, on the river Darent in Kent, England, there are six little mills which for nearly three hundred years had produced paper which had won that reputation. Everyone in the vicinity of Eynsford worked in one of these mills, in several instances grandfather, father, and son. Papermaking was a tradition. They lived it and breathed it, and the pride of workmanship which went into the finished product gave it the quality it possessed. William Morris selected this type of paper for the "Kelmscott Chaucer," and it was obvious that this was the paper I must have for the Subscription Edition of Science and Health.

My requirements caused some complications which had to be straightened out. In the first place, I required a larger sheet than they had ever manufactured, so large, in fact, that the mold in which the paper was made required four men to lift the screen after it had been immersed and shaken in the vat. The making of this mold itself required two months, and in addition I insisted upon having the Cross and Crown introduced as a watermark in addition to the famous watermark of the manufacturer, which was the hallmark of its quality.

The order was accepted, and the work started,

when I received a cable to the effect that the British
Government, now at war, had commandeered all six
of these little mills for the purpose of manufacturing
paper for percussion caps for shells. To have this
cancellation would have been disastrous. Reaching high
up into the zone of influence, we succeeded in impressing upon the British Government the importance
of the volume for which the paper was being manufactured, with the result that they graciously counter-
manded their order as affecting this particular mill,
holding up their war demands until after this special
lot of paper had been run.

So the manufacturing continued with strict regard
to my injunctions, all the conditions of which were
successfully met, including the uniform thickness which
was necessary to keep the bulk of the volume at a
fixed three inches.

Then came the transportation of the paper across
an ocean infested with U-boats. The shipping was
done in four installments, and if any one of these four
had been lost, it would have been disastrous for the
undertaking, for when the original order was once run
at the mill, the British Government immediately took
over. Happily, however, all four shipments arrived
safely.

When it came to the matter of presswork, I
employed the same methods as in setting the type,
selecting a pressman who had appealed to me as a man

unusually interested in his work. I took him into my confidence, and explained that instead of merely producing a book, we were trying to create a masterpiece, and that his contribution was of paramount importance. I took him to the Boston Public Library and showed him the beautiful "Racine" printed by Firmin Didot in Paris in 1801, which I consider the finest example of presswork in the world. I called his attention to the care with which the printer of that book prepared his forms of type so that the impression just bites into the surface of the paper, becoming a part of the paper itself and preserving a uniform, unbroken color.

When the work actually started, I again emphasized the fact that the element of time was to be completely disregarded. Ordinarily, when a pressman receives his slip, the foreman has intimated on it the amount of time he estimates that particular order should require. In this case the slip was simply filled in "Pressman to use his own discretion." When the pressman saw this, he was deeply affected. Turning to me, he said, "All my life I have hoped to have an order placed in my hands without any limit of time, and at last I have that gratification." The actual presswork of the book required nine months to produce the one thousand copies.

The matter of ink was carefully studied. The layman does not realize how many shades there are to black ink, and in printing a book the nature of the paper and the adaptability of the ink require careful consideration. The black ink selected was made of the finest ingredients known. The red ink required even more careful consideration, as red is subject to fading. I sought the co-operation of one of the leading printing-ink manufacturers, and explained to him that I wanted to secure an ink which matched in every way the medieval red which the old-time painters used to make for their own use. With his help we succeeded in getting exactly what I wanted, and secured a shade of red which I have never seen duplicated, and which, after the severest tests, has proved permanent in color.

The binding required long and careful study. Ordinarily on a book this size, which requires a particularly large skin, binders find it necessary to piece the leather, joining it in the "gutter" which separates the shelfback from the recto and verso. I wanted to avoid this. Morocco is goatskin, and the largest goats are to be found in India. Here skins were obtained of a size to bind the volume without piecing it, and the order was placed.

Now we had to face the same perils of war which surrounded the transportation of the paper. First of all, the skins had to be shipped by water from India to London for processing and dyeing. There is a firm in London which does this processing in such a way that the permanence of the dye is guaranteed, and the commission went to them. The skins were shipped in ten lots of one hundred each, and again came the deep concern of piloting these ten shipments from India to London and from London to Boston without loss due to U-boat attack. When the tenth shipment finally arrived, a great load of responsibility was lifted from my mind.

Then came the matter of stamping. The lettering was made to match in every respect the Laurentian design of the type to be found inside on the printed pages. Brass dies were cut, and the first sample covers that were stamped had the lettering in gold. This was the conventional thing to do, but, when Mr. Burr and I saw these covers, we realized that the contrast between the brilliant gold of the letters and the deep, beautiful dull blue of the leather placed the accent too strongly on the lettering. It was another case of two beautiful things, the leather and the lettering, competing against each other, and the lettering had to be modified by impressing it in blank so as to make it a part of the leather itself. This also avoided the criticism Mrs. Eddy had made of the Morris books. She felt that the beauty of the type and the beauty of the deco- rations competed against each other, and thus "ruined for its own the common cause."

Thus in June, 1941, the Subscription Edition of Science and Health was completed — a project thirty- eight years in conception, eighteen months in production. Never was a volume started during a period more fraught with threatened complications, never was a volume that moved more smoothly from start to finish. Difficulties raised their heads only to eliminate themselves before thwarting the progress of the work. Each participant called in to play his part proved to be the exact person best fitted to perform it; each component part when combined with the others demonstrated the "rightness" of the selection.

All this could not have been mere coincidence.

Nearly a decade has passed since the publication of this edition. During that period not one copy has been returned for any defect — no torn leaf, no type mistake, no scratched binding.

All this is beyond the reward for careful workmanship.

Could it not be that there was another unseen but beneficent influence that guided the book throughout the various processes with a certainty more powerful than we know, and that the serenity of the atmosphere through which it passed was an assurance of the "rightness" of the undertaking?

I like to think so, and I shall always think so.

L'Envoi

L'Envoi

A QUESTION that is frequently put to me by Christian Science acquaintances who have learned of my long association with Mrs. Eddy is, "Were you conscious of Mrs. Eddy's unusual attributes when in her presence?" If by that question the suggestion is that she gave outward evidence of possessing characteristics setting her apart from worldly association, the answer is definitely in the negative. Mrs. Eddy was first and foremost a woman, and a very human woman. That she could express so much humanity and still possess the spirituality she manifested is what made so deep an impression upon me. There were so many little kindly acts and thoughtful gestures which cannot be put into written words, but remain printed on the tablets of the mind or impressed upon the inner shrine of the heart.

That I was always conscious of being in the presence of a remarkable woman is a definite fact. As I look back, the greatness of her qualities became progressively more apparent. The early respect became admiration, the friendship developed into affection. If I were to describe her I might say that she was dignified, but not aloof; friendly, but not intimate; kindly, but not demonstrative; determined, but not stubborn.

I have seen the demand for the textbook develop from thousands into millions. I have witnessed Mrs. Eddy's message spread over the face of the earth. I have seen her personality become a continuing, living force, even to thousands who never saw her. But somehow, when I think of her, it is not as a world celebrity or as the founder of a great religious movement. Instead, it is that earliest impression at Pleasant View that comes back to me — acres of green grass, a placid little lake, a silver strip of river, and a boundary line of hills. And within the unpretentious house a slight, unassuming, kindly woman — very real, very human, very appealing, supremely content in the self-knowledge that no matter what others might think, she was delivering her message to the world.

Index

Index